LIKE WATER

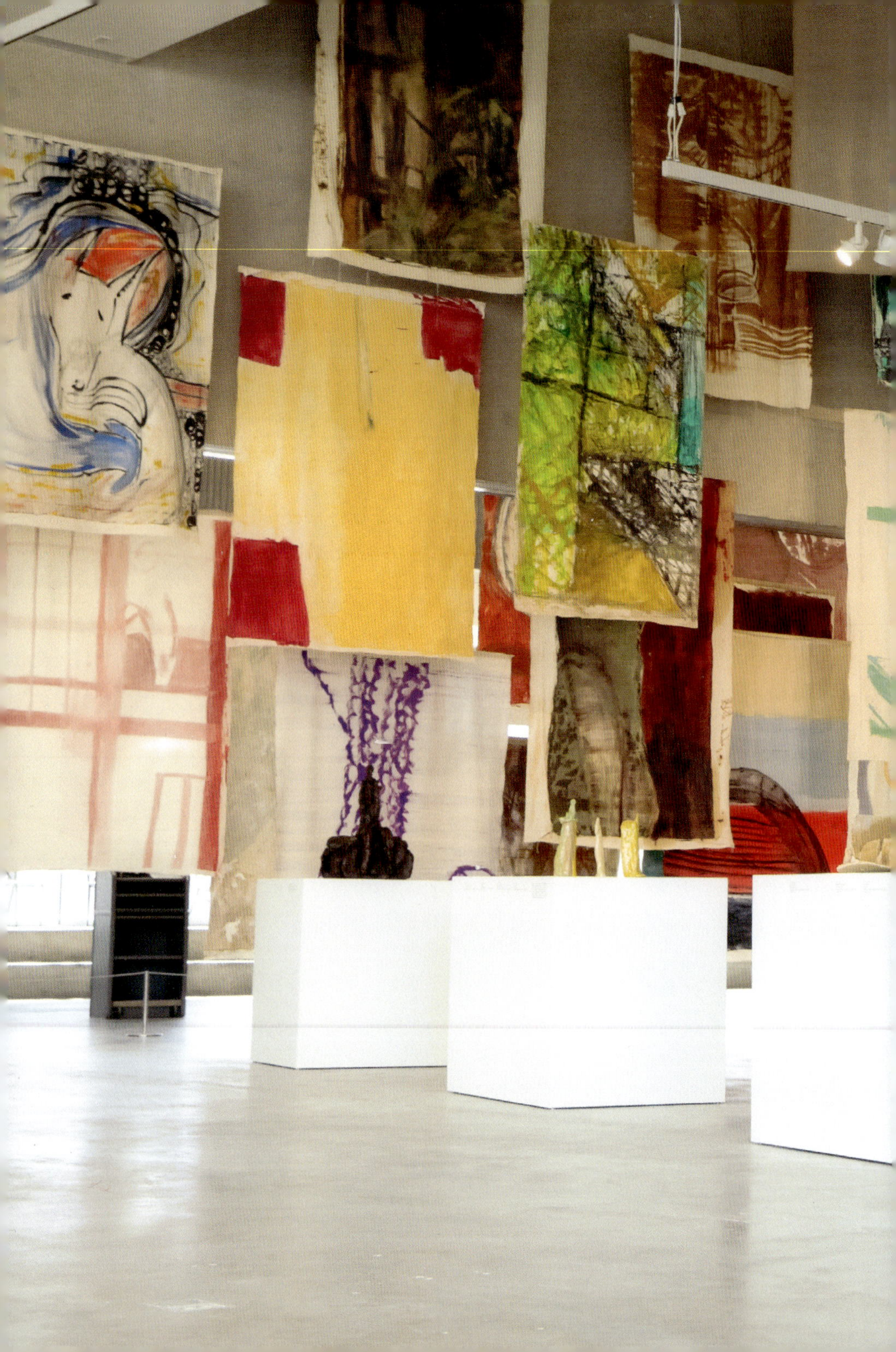

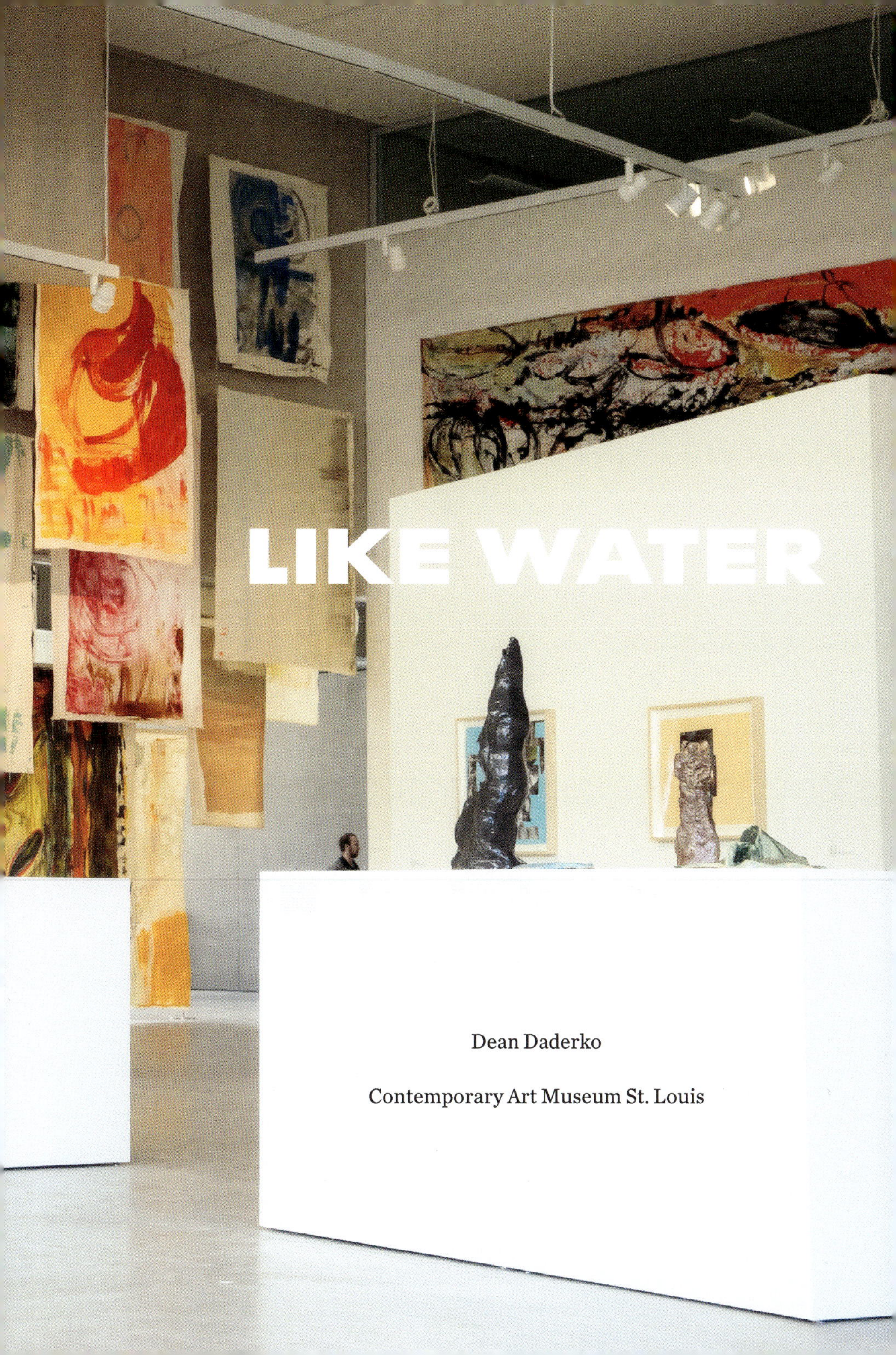

LIKE WATER

Dean Daderko

Contemporary Art Museum St. Louis

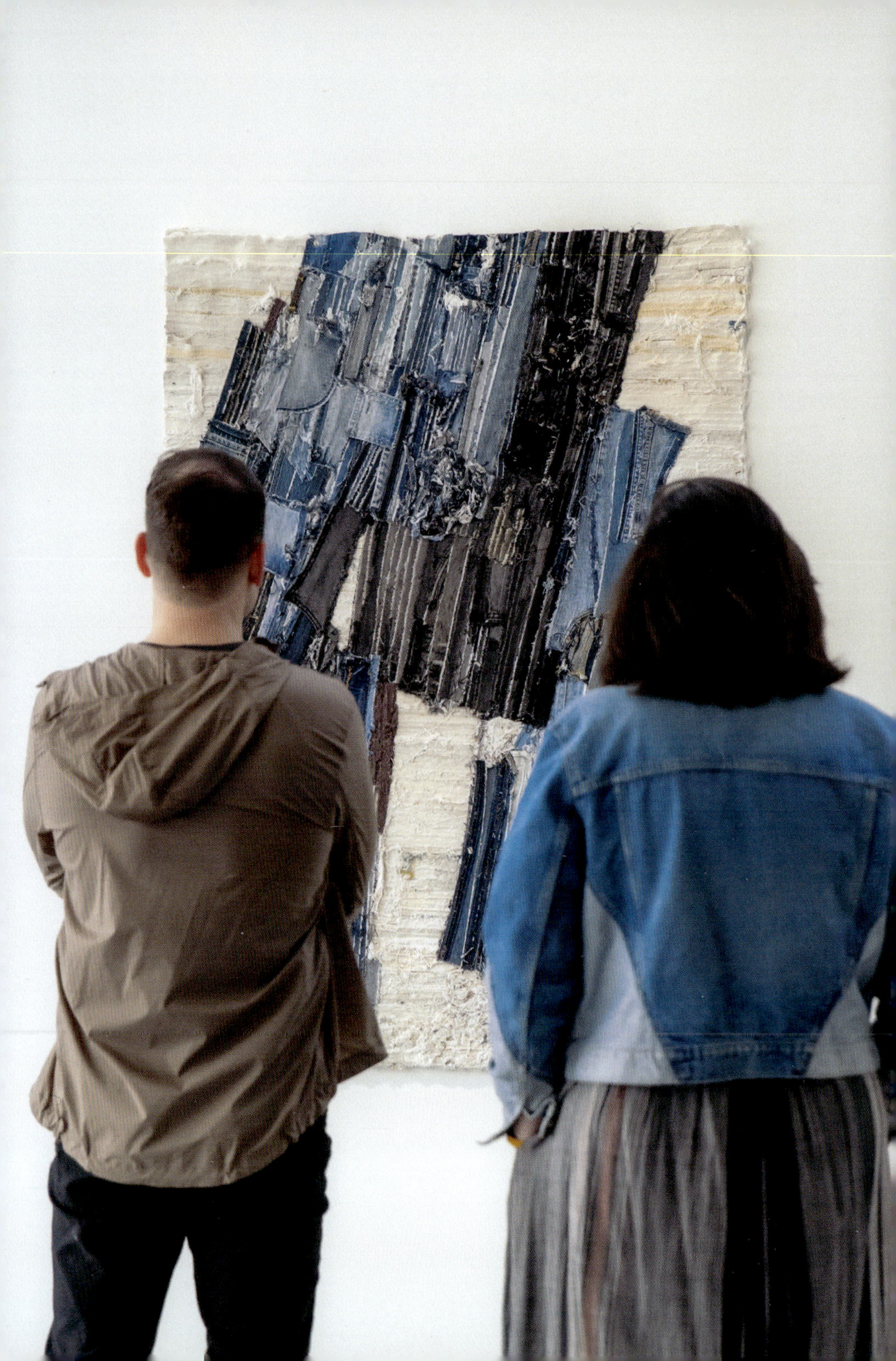

CONTENTS

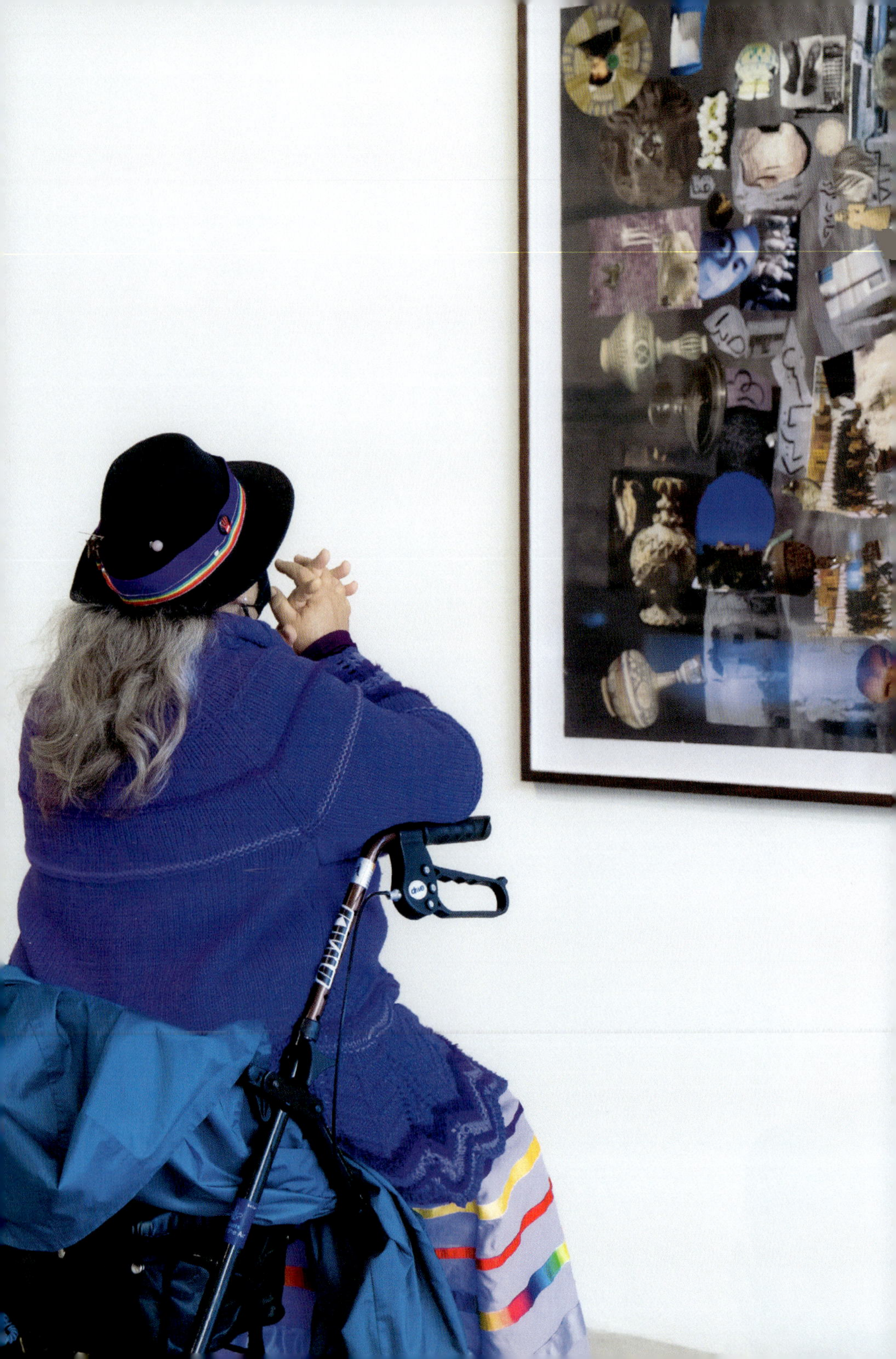

FOREWORD

Like Water brought together a multigenerational group of artists working in the US and abroad whose artworks center the emotional, metaphorical, and poetic depths of water. Jamal Cyrus, Simone Fattal, Dionne Lee, Candice Lin, Beatriz Santiago Muñoz, and Vivian Suter work in a rich variety of mediums, including sculpture, video, ceramics, installation, drawing, textile, collage, and painting. Their work references a wide array of topics related to the definition and idea of water from the Middle Passage, US colonial political structures and trade relationships, abstraction and representation, underground currents and cultural histories, fluidity and poetry. *Like Water* offered CAM's visitors, and now the readers of this publication, the opportunity to reflect on the cultural, ecological, and sociopolitical ecosystems in which we all circulate.

Ferring Foundation Chief Curator Dean Daderko's vision in bringing together this compelling array of artists and artworks is emblematic of their thoughtful approach to recognizing artistic connections. Kevin Harris, Exhibitions Production and A/V Specialist, and Grace Early, Exhibitions Assistant, brought their efforts and expertise to the coordination of this exhibition. Jen Nugent, former Registrar and Exhibition Production Manager started the work and planning for this project, and its continuation was adeptly handled by Erica Buss, current Registrar and Exhibition Production Manager. Numerous other members of the Contemporary Art Museum St. Louis's staff helped bring *Like Water* to fruition, and we thank them for their efforts. Marquand Books and D.A.P. / Distributed Art Publishers have expertly produced and distributed this book.

In addition to our in-house staff, I offer my sincerest thanks to those who supported the exhibition and this publication: The Andy Warhol Foundation for the Visual Arts; Étant donnés; Independent Curators International; Alison Sieloff and Sam Foxman; Edward Jones; Missouri Arts Council, a state agency with funding from the National Endowment for the Arts; Emily Rauh Pulitzer; Ann R. Ruwitch and John Fox Arnold; Mary Ann and Andy Srenco; Pat Whitaker and Dick Miles; and Whitaker Foundation. Our appreciation also goes to Katharine Barthelme Frank and Shane Frank, P.Bibeau, Rona and Jeff Citrin, Kathleen Frumkin and George Lakoff, François Ghebaly, Gladstone Gallery, Carol Greene, Inman Gallery, Karma International, kaufmann repetto, Modern Art Museum of Forth Worth, and Sociedad del Tiempo Libre for lending works to *Like Water*.

We are also deeply grateful to the participating artists—Jamal Cyrus, Simone Fattal, Dionne Lee, Candice Lin, Beatriz Santiago Muñoz, and Vivian Suter—for their extraordinary creative vision. It was an honor to exhibit their work in this dynamic confluence.

Lisa Melandri
Executive Director

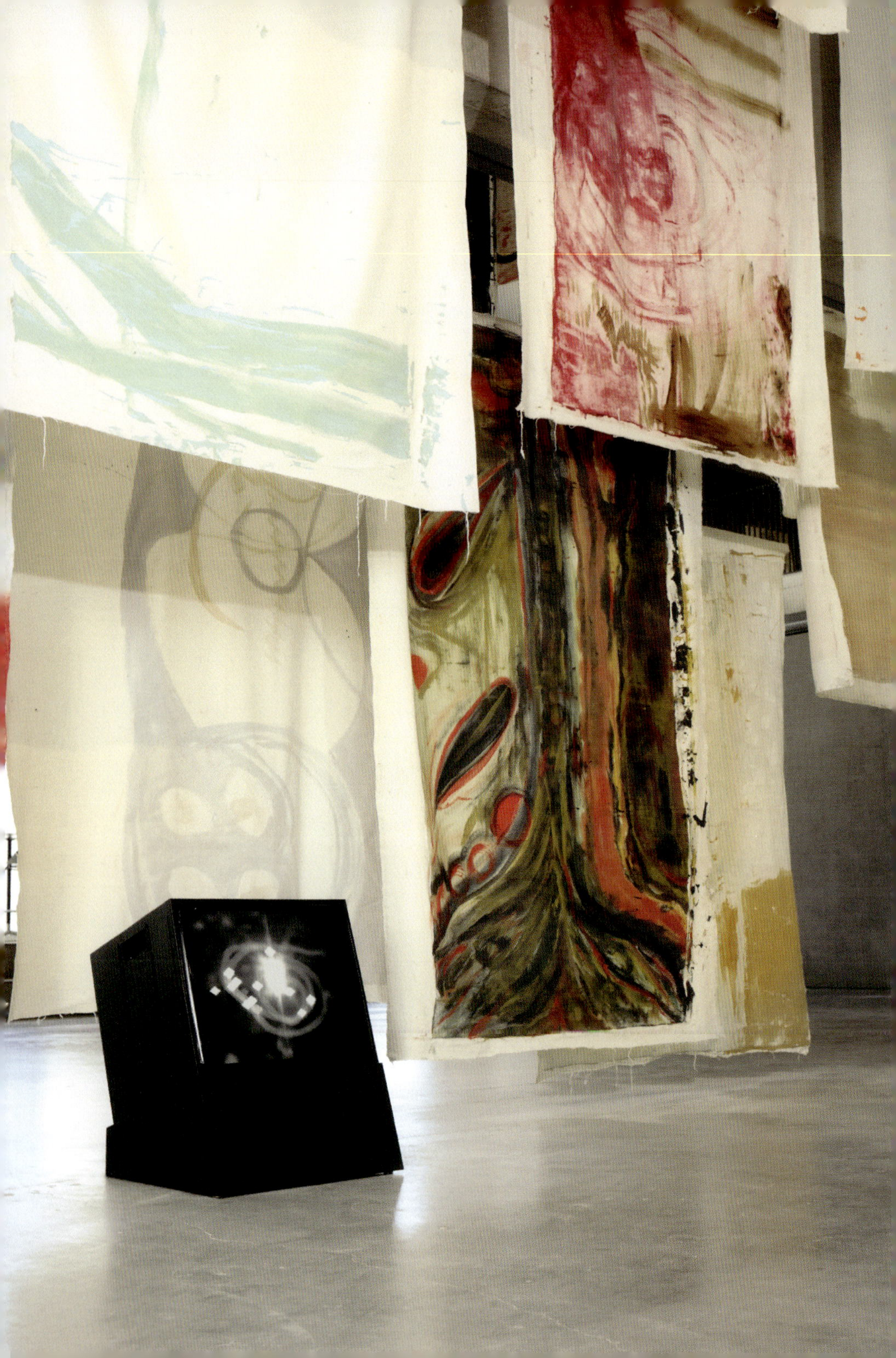

ACKNOWLEDGMENTS

Like Water was realized with support from many individuals and organizations, and I am pleased to have the opportunity to recognize their contributions.

Major support for *Like Water* was provided by The Andy Warhol Foundation for the Visual Arts. Generous support was also provided by Étant donnés, a program of the Villa Albertine; Independent Curators International through a Mississippi River Basin Curatorial Research Fellowship; Alison Sieloff and Sam Foxman; Emily Rauh Pulitzer; Ann R. Ruwitch and John Fox Arnold; Mary Ann and Andy Srenco; Pat Whitaker and Dick Miles; and Whitaker Foundation. The unwavering interest of CAM's Board of Directors and the Museum's supporters fosters our continuing success.

My deepest gratitude is due to the participating artists—Jamal Cyrus, Simone Fattal, Dionne Lee, Candice Lin, Beatriz Santiago Muñoz, and Vivian Suter—for their support and enthusiasm as *Like Water* came together.

Thanks are also due to the lenders and galleries who entrusted the museum with artworks: Katharine Barthelme Frank and Shane

Frank; Petra Bibeau and P.Bibeau; Rona and Jeff Citrin; Kathleen Frumkin and George Lakoff; François Ghebaly, New York and Los Angeles; Frederik Schampers and Gladstone Gallery, New York; Kerry Inman and Inman Gallery, Houston; Justine Hauer and Karma International, Zurich; Chiara Repetto, Davide Pirovano and kaufmann repetto, Milan and New York; Modern Art Museum of Fort Worth, Texas; Mary Coyne and PATRON Gallery, Chicago; and Sociedad del Tiempo Libre, San Juan, Puerto Rico. Thanks to Sam Pribish in Dionne Lee's studio, and Valentina Suma in Simone Fattal's studio for their kind assistance; to Gan Uyeda for support of Candice Lin's project; and to K. Curtis Lyle, Corey De'Juan Sherrard, Jr., and Damon Smith for their contributions to Jamal Cyrus's performance *Horn Beam Sacrament*. Colleagues at Marquand Books brought insight and discernment to the realization of the publication you are holding.

My gratitude goes to my colleagues at the Contemporary Art Museum St. Louis, who have each brought their time, talents, work, and vision to securing funding, public attention, and opportunities for our community to engage with *Like Water* during its run. As always, thanks to Executive Director Lisa Melandri for her keen perspectives and enthusiasm. Among others, I want to recognize Erica Buss, Chris Carl, Grace Early, Kevin Harris, Misa Jeffereis, Jen Nugent, and the installation crew for *Like Water* for their contributions.

Finally, thanks to Alhena Katsof, Daisy Nam, Ulrike Müller, and Renaud Proch for ongoing conversations that helped to shape this exhibition.

Dean Daderko
Ferring Foundation Chief Curator

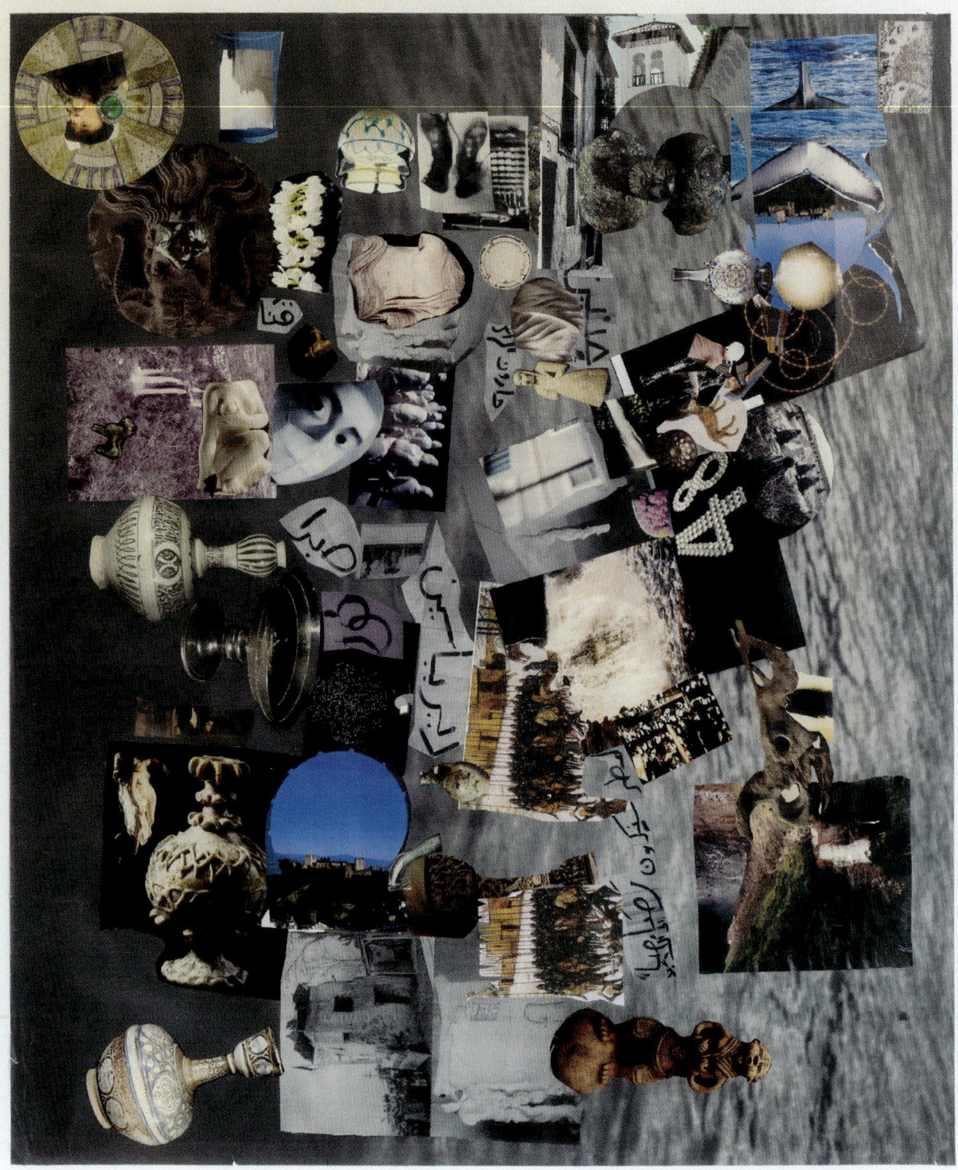

LIKE WATER

Dean Daderko

In *Like Water*, landscape is simultaneously understood as a physical material condition and an interior, emotional state. Across substantive selections of artworks by Jamal Cyrus, Simone Fattal, Dionne Lee, Candice Lin, Beatriz Santiago Muñoz and Vivian Suter, water is explored in its wide variety of material, poetic, narrative, and abstract capacities. Animating this exhibition, constellations of connections intermix across audio tracks, ceramics, collages, drawing, installation, painting, performance, photography, sculptures, and textiles. Groups of selected artworks are united by considerations of colonial power in the United States and further afield. Gesture is another undercurrent, as is the notion of the undercurrent itself, which moves invisibly yet is sensed nonetheless. In this way, water is revealed as a metaphoric carrier of information, taking the shape of the vessels and spaces it fills. And as water is elementally and environmentally necessary for all organisms and ecosystems here on Earth, *Like Water* equally celebrates art as a form of communication and expression that can itself feed and nourish us.

Simone Fattal, *Le Grand Renversement 1948* [The Great Reversal 1948], 2012. Collage, 45 × 38 inches.

Courtesy the artist and Karma International, Zurich. Photo: Flavio Karrer.

When we're navigating complex and layered emotional terrain, we often talk about experiencing "floods of emotion." We may describe profound sensations that seem to exceed the physical limitations of our bodies as "fonts of inspiration." Like terrestrial sources of water arriving from unknown origins, experiences can seem to exceed the physical limitations of our bodies, flowing through and out of us. As such, it's not surprising that the etymological source is the Latin word for spring–*font* or *fons*. Hosts of other examples exist: We say we feel "under water" or that we're struggling to keep our heads above it when feeling challenged. Tears of sadness and joy often accompany an emotional overflow. Water's metaphors are deep. With a clarity that can verge on invisibility and a liquidity that avoids fixed form, water can be aptly compared to emotions.

Water follows the path of least resistance. It slips through our fingers, soaks into the ground, hydrates what it touches, and evaporates into the air. For all of the ways that water can be difficult to measure, life as we know it on Earth is dependent on ample sources of clean, uncontaminated water. While human exploration has touched most of our dry lands, the depths of the Earth's oceans remain among the most mysterious and elusive places on this planet. The National Oceanic and Atmospheric Association reports that only 25 percent of ocean floors have been mapped, leaving the majority of ocean floors "largely unknown." Even though sonar can be used to picture these places, much remains unexplored and beyond our grasp, at least by present humankind. In this way, water offers another kind of invisibility: one of incredible pressure, impenetrable to sunlight. Here, water's force is tremendous and crushing. In fact, water has done more to terraform or shape the earth than any other element. Even as it erodes and reshapes landscapes in ways that can be painfully harsh, water also has the welcome power to influence the world around us in ways that are gentle and incredibly subtle.

Prior to moving to St. Louis, I expected I would use the Mississippi River to orient myself as I navigated through this city. As such, it was surprising to recognize the relative *invisibility* of the river within this city's urban landscape. Part of this is, of course, geographic: Surrounded by relatively flat plains, the river cuts a deep channel, so it's not often in plain sight. Known most broadly as the Mississippi

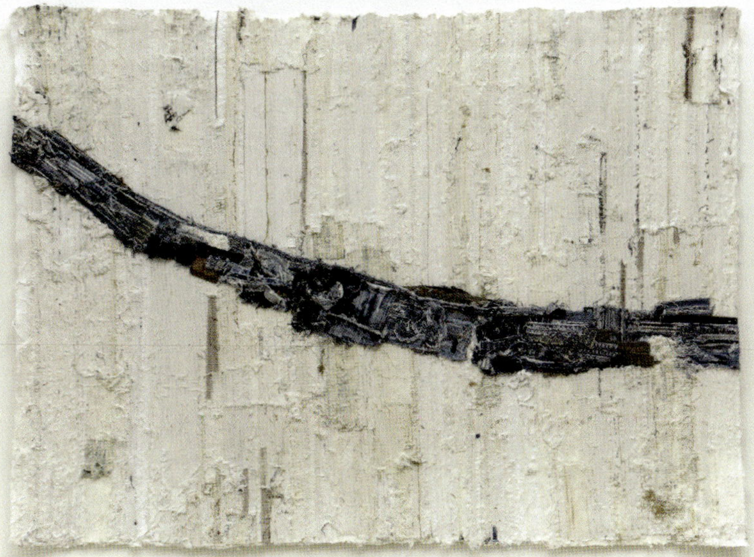

Embayment, these plains house some of the most agriculturally fertile farmland in the Midwest. Horizons here lay low. The Mississippi's absence from view is equally the result of the privatization of its banks by modern industry. Lined with barges, tugboats, and processing facilities, much material makes its way to the river to be shipped both down- and upstream.

Thousands of years ago, before the Mississippi and the Missouri Rivers were controlled by manmade locks and dams, these two rivers (and many others) flooded their banks seasonally. In the spring, melting snow and rains muddied tributary creeks and filled smaller streams, flowing onward into increasingly larger and more powerful rivers. The Mississippi is popularly known by the more recent nickname "Big Muddy," but for some Indigenous peoples, the word *Mississippi* meant "the great river" or "the gathering-in of all waters." The word *Missouri* derives from *8emessourit,* an Algonquian term that refers to "people with canoes (made from logs)." Prior to (and after) the colonization of the United States, these rivers functioned as liquid highways, orienting the way-finding of scores of Indigenous peoples who gathered

Jamal Cyrus, *Blue Alluvial Glue 2 (Line)*, 2022. Denim, cotton thread, cotton batting, metal, 42 ½ × 55 inches.

Collection of the Modern Art Museum of Fort Worth, Gift of the Director's Council and Museum Purchase, 2022. Courtesy the Modern Art Museum of Fort Worth. Photo: Kevin Todora.

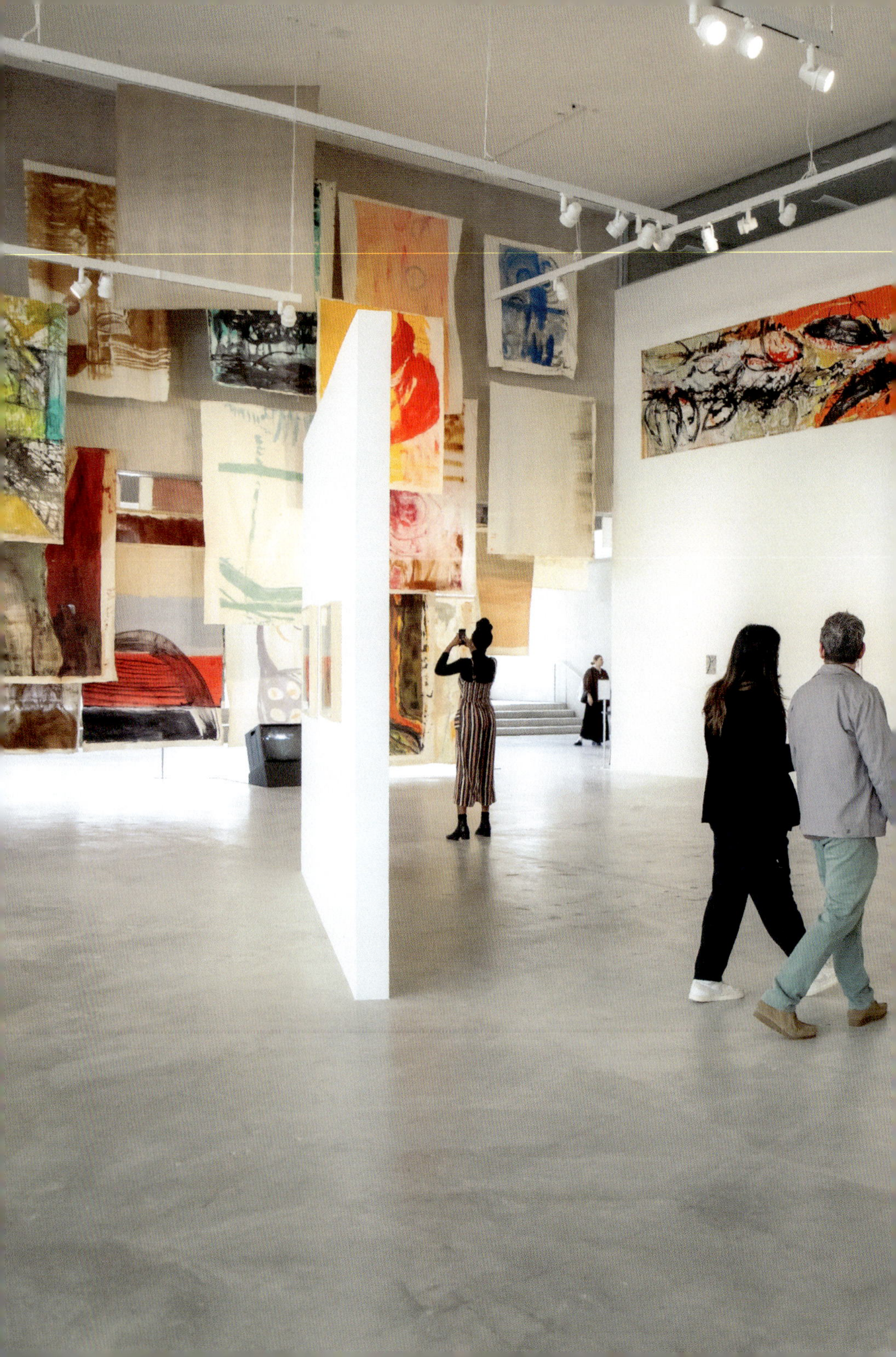

here both permanently and seasonally. Periodic flooding by the Mississippi and Missouri Rivers certainly brought destruction, but it also fed the land by laying down the sedimentary layers on alluvial plains that made this area agriculturally fertile and fostered habitation of people, flora, and fauna. Notably, the land just south of the confluence of the Mississippi and Missouri Rivers was home to the largest pre-Columbian human settlement north of Mexico, and the largest prehistoric earthen structure built in either North or South America. At its peak between 1050 and 1150, an estimated 20,000 people lived in community in and around the famed mounds of Cahokia, forming a cultural, religious, and economic center that rivaled the contemporaneous populations of cities like London and Paris. Mississippian culture existed from 800 to 1350, and the fact that human habitation of this region predates European colonization adds further layers of depth to the complex, rich history of this area.

The Mississippi's vast circulatory system connects more than half of the United States. This riparian landscape directly affects the lives of those living in and around it. Pulling back further, the river and other landscapes like it offer a mirror for physical and emotional wellbeing. Care for the environment is a demonstration of holistic priorities: How we care for the land shows how we care for ourselves. Moving such narratives forward, the artists in *Like Water* share stories about and through this vital substance. In their works, viewers are offered opportunities to consider regional ecologies, material and environmental realities, changing histories, and the richness of the cultural, natural, and sociopolitical ecosystems in which we circulate.

b. 1979, Concord, MA. Lives and works in Los Angeles, CA

CANDICE LIN establishes opportunities for buried, overlooked narratives to be unearthed and teased. Unfolding in alchemical and (pseudo)scientific ways, Lin has referred to her works as "tactile theaters." *La Charada China* (2018/2025) is one such installation. In the center of a room with an earthen floor sits a mound into which a human silhouette has been excavated. Dirt fills these craters, and a mix of seeds has been planted into them that includes buffalo grass, false indigo, and sugarcane. A series of altars rings the room's outer edges and one appears at the central mound's base. The surrounding walls are sheathed in rippling silver Mylar that reflects and amplifies the glow

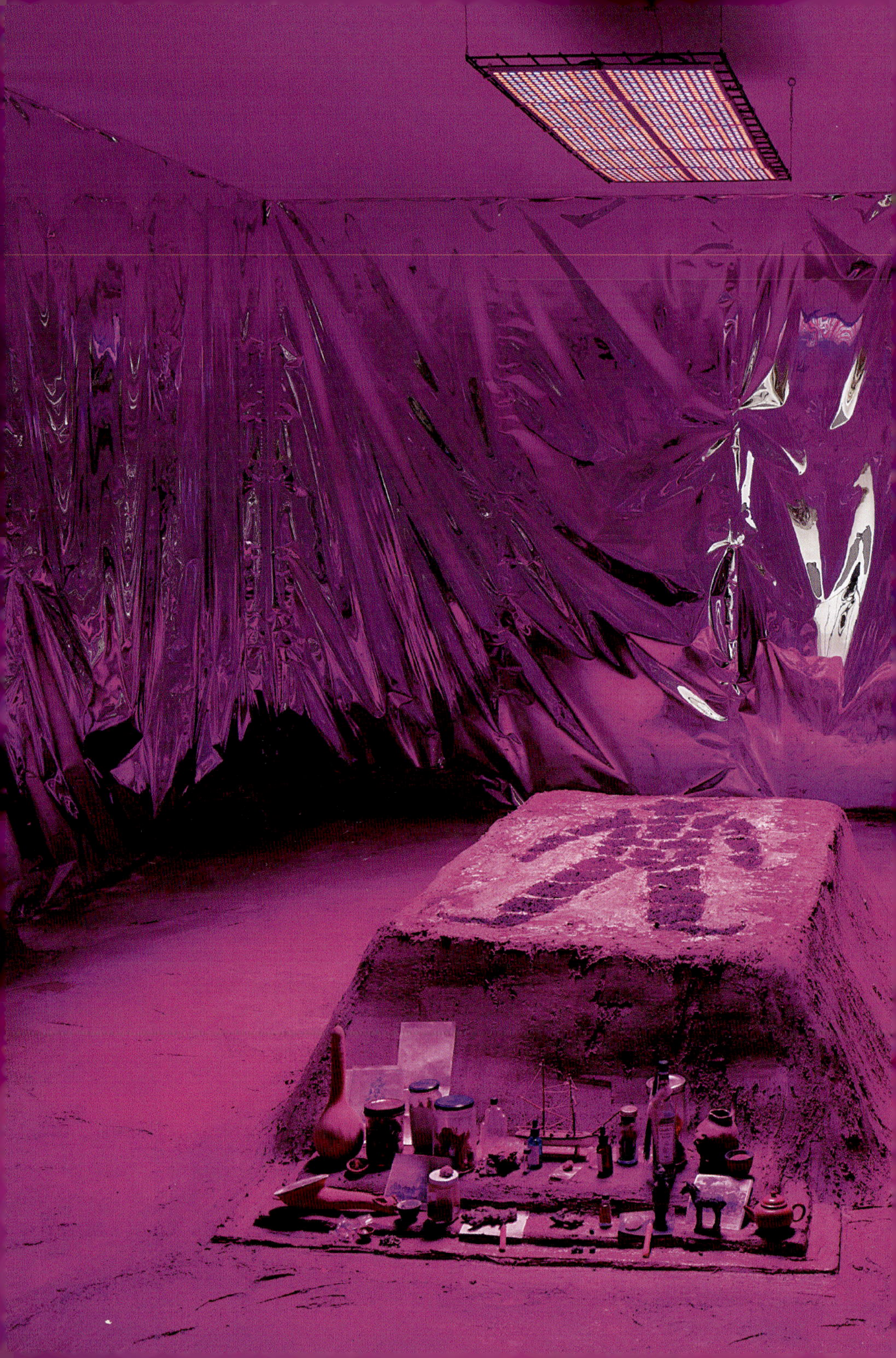

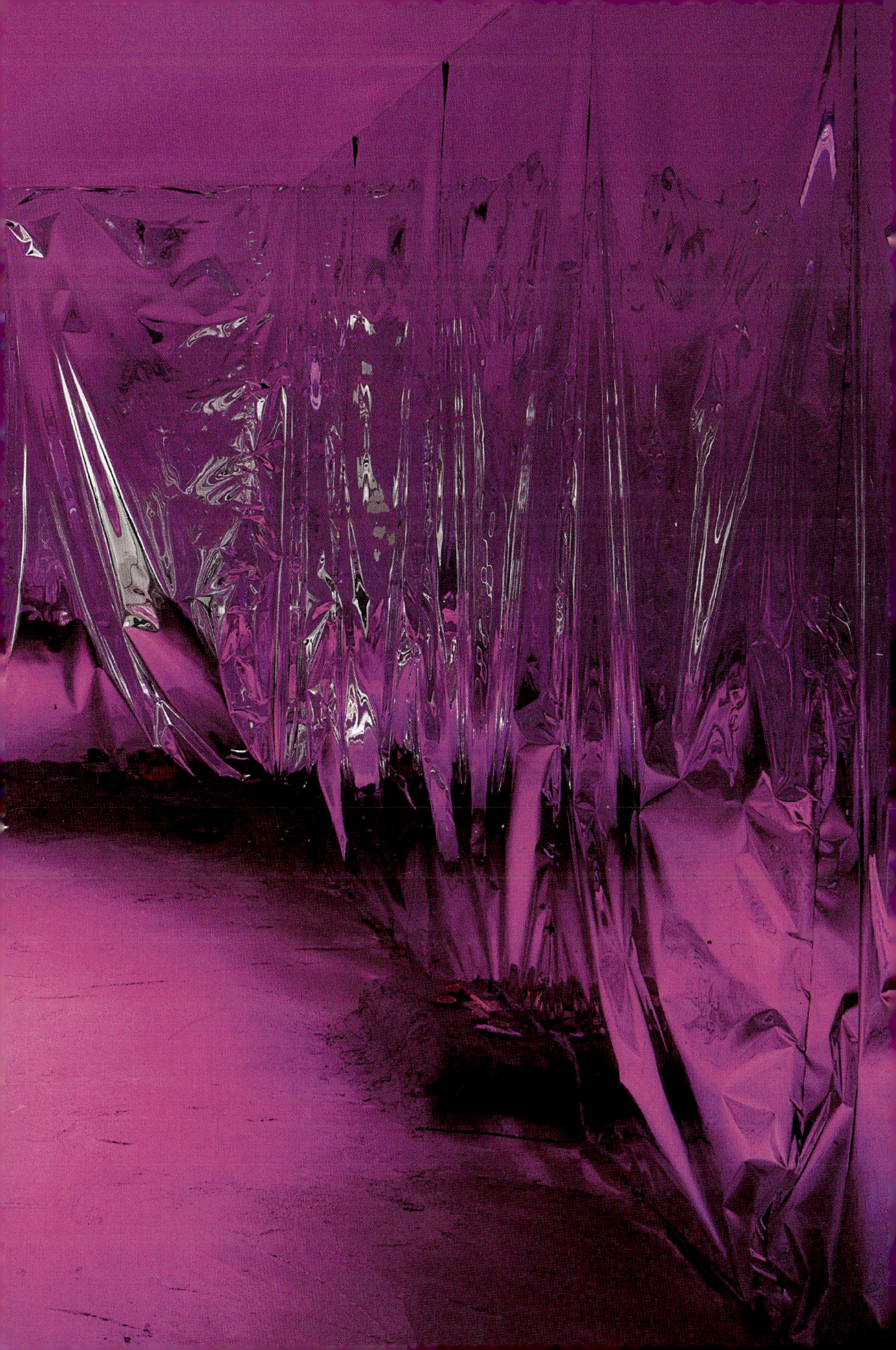

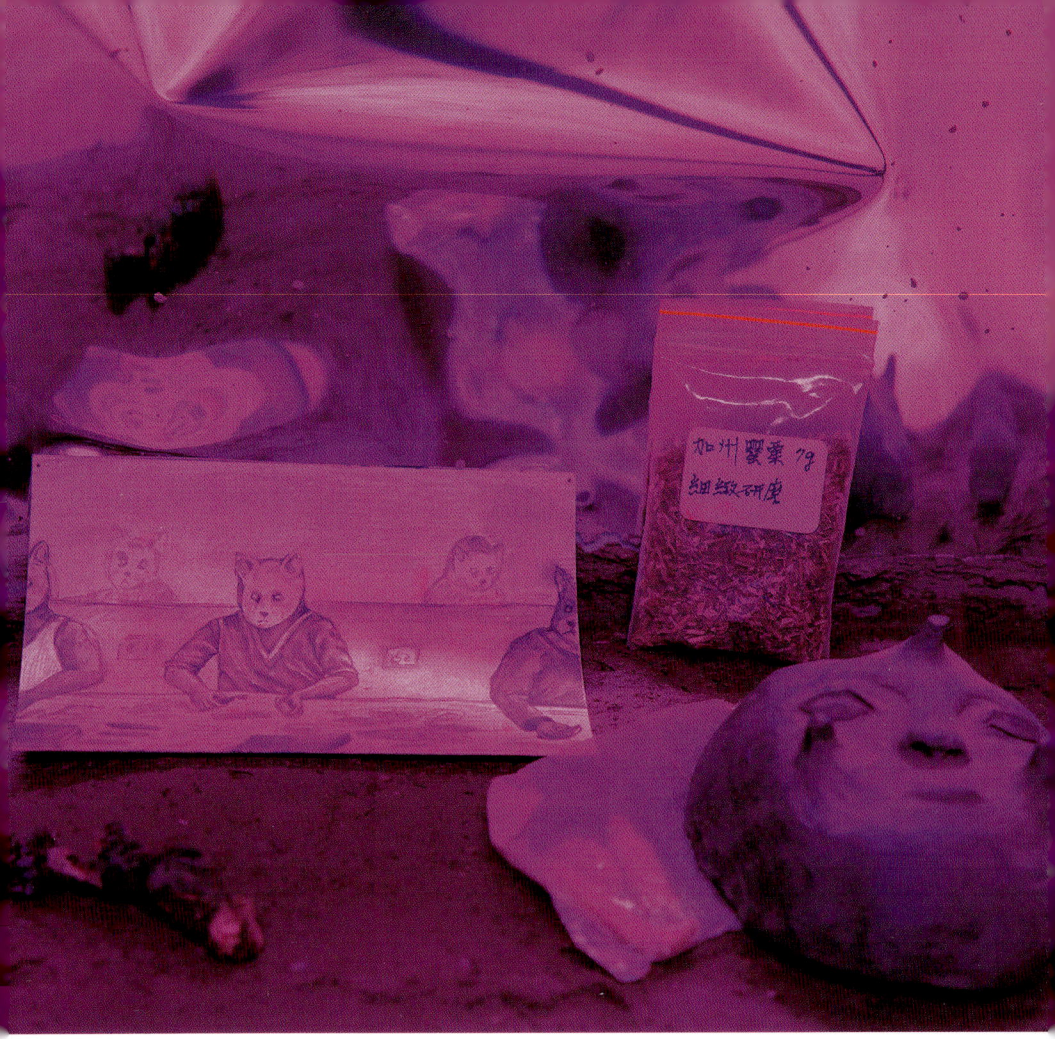

Candice Lin, *La Charada China* (detail) and previous, 2018/2025. Earth, red clay, guano, cement, poppy seeds, sugarcane, seeds of various poisonous Caribbean plants, grow light, Mylar, wooden and metal armature, soaker hoses, irrigation system, tinctures in glass bottles, ceramics, toy boat, gourds, pencil on paper drawings, teapots, teacups, photographs, dried flora, chain, hardware, audio (11:47 minutes).

Courtesy the artist and François Ghebaly, Los Angeles and New York. Photo: Izaiah Johnson.

of a pink grow light hanging from the ceiling. It nurtures germinating seeds, and gives the room a psychedelic edge, offering back trippy and destabilizing reflections.

This presentation of Lin's *La Charada China* incorporates a new audio soundtrack. In it, the artist nods to Louisa May Alcott (1832–1888), the American author born in Concord, Massachusetts, nearly a century before Lin herself was born there. Across a series of fluid identifications and historical anecdotes, the narrator imagines herself as a horse and a dismantled Chinese house being shipped overseas. Lin was drawn to Alcott's historical moment as a time in which objects from Asia were beginning to be imported into the United States, fueling fantasies of unknown lands and people.

The installation's title is a reference to a still-popular Cuban card game that's a graphic variant of roulette. This gambling metaphor is fitting, as it reflects the risks taken by Chinese immigrants who emigrated into indentured servitude, risking their lives to acquire a better future. According to the artist:

> *La Charada China is a syncretic gambling game that draws from a host of symbolic systems—Spanish Lotería cards, Chinese astrology, African Yoruban gods, and Indigenous folklore. It mapped these symbols onto a stereotyped figure of a Chinese man in elfin slippers with a long braided queue of hair who holds an opium pipe in his left hand. In the 19th century Chinese laborers gathered around gambling games like this one in communities of hope and chance. While no single laborer could earn enough money to exit a system of debt-peonage that was stacked against them, the game gathered a pool of money from everyone and redistributed it to one lucky winner, enabling that person to return to China or to stay in the U.S. or Caribbean, open a store, make a home and settle down.*

La Charada China pays homage to scores of Chinese indentured laborers who were brought to the Caribbean and the American South in the 1800s to replace or supplement enslaved workers on farms and in construction trades, where many died. Throughout the room, the altars filled with ceramics, teapots, a toy boat, drawings, photographs,

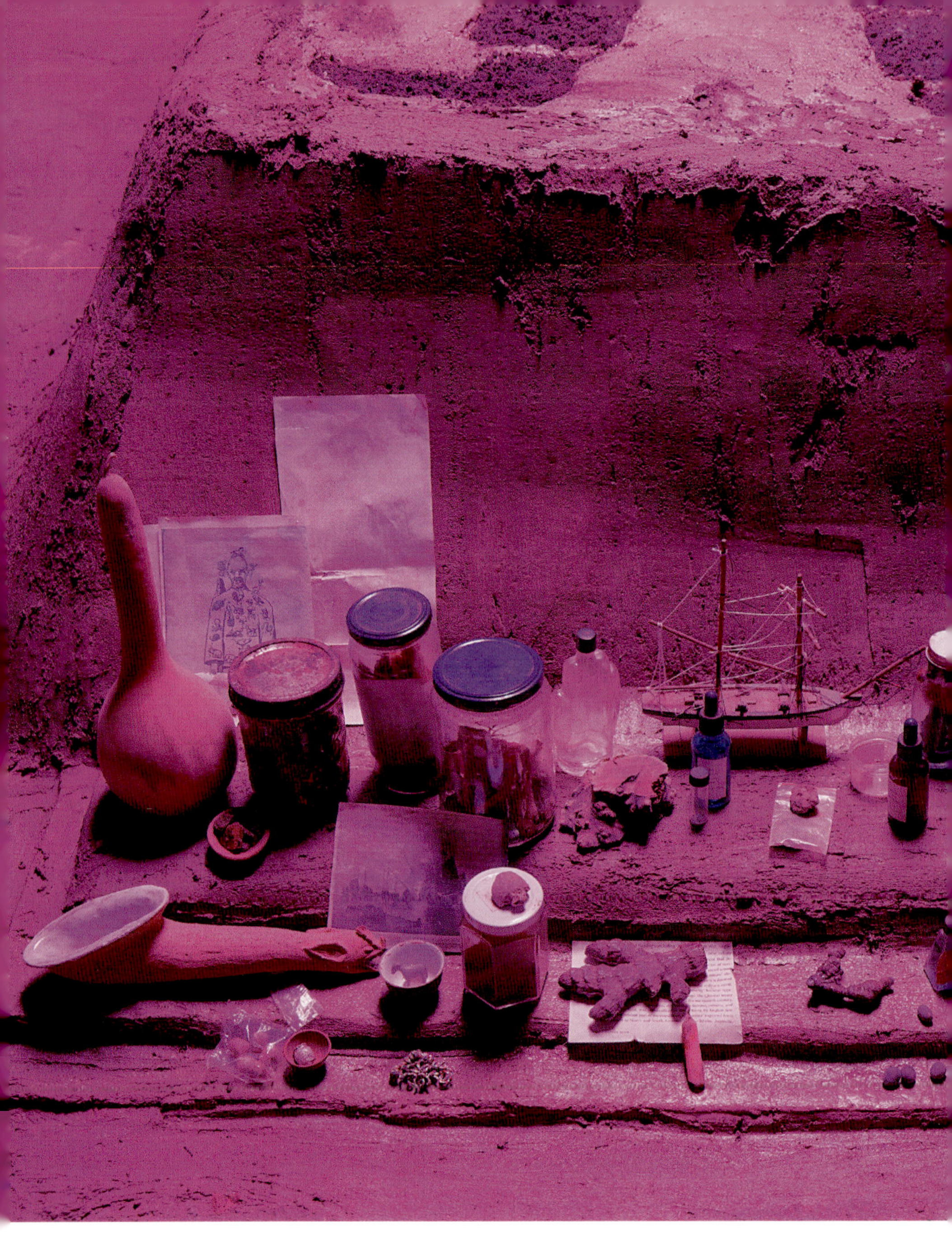

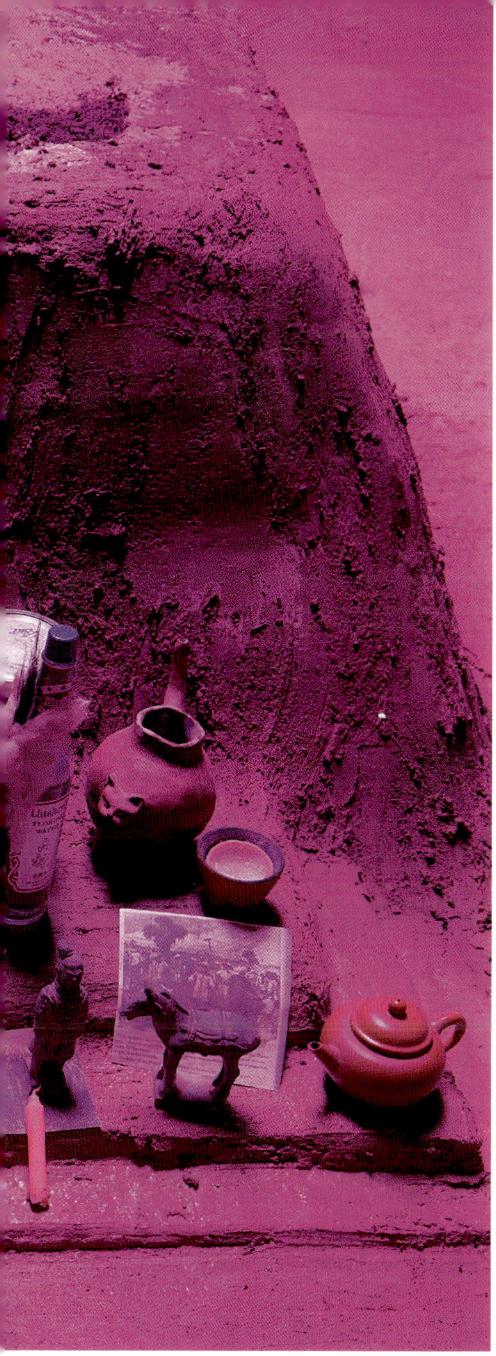

Candice Lin, *La Charada China* (detail), 2018/2025.

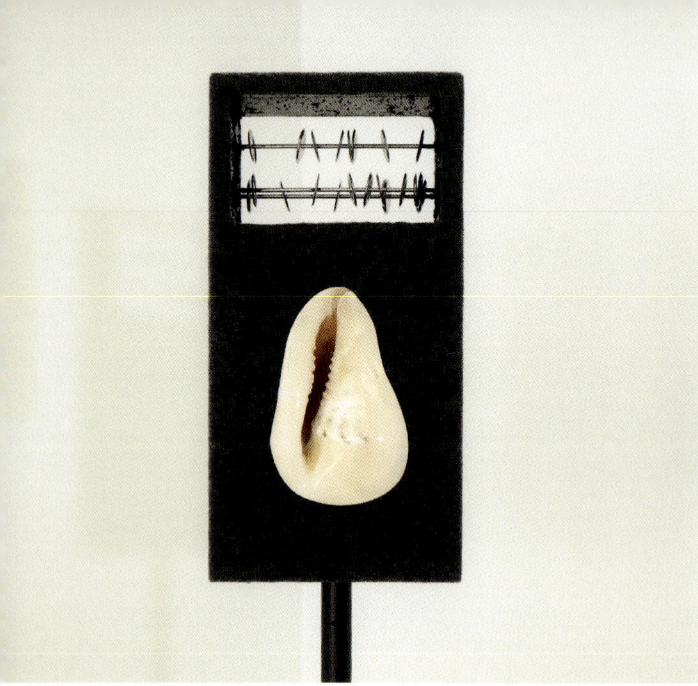

Jamal Cyrus, *Sstrum* (detail), 2022. Helmet conch shell, wood, carpet, speaker stand, tambourine zills, corn grits, India ink, 75 × 18 × 15 inches.

Photo: Izaiah Johnson.

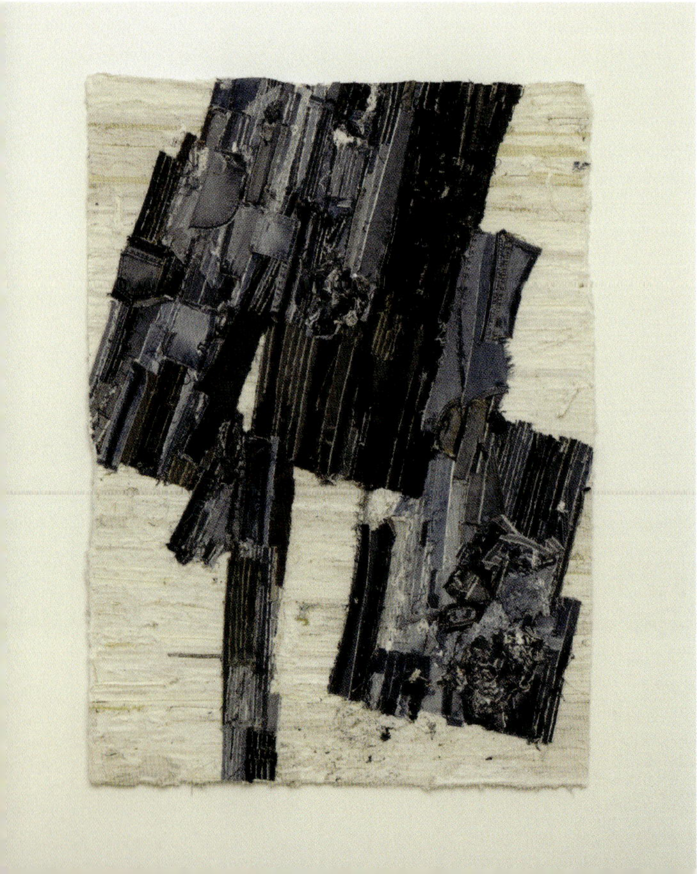

Jamal Cyrus, *Blue Alluvial Glue 1 (Shape)*, 2022. Denim, cotton thread, cotton batting, 56 × 42 inches.

Collection of the Modern Art Museum of Fort Worth, Gift of the Director's Council and Museum purchase, 2022. Courtesy the Modern Art Museum of Fort Worth. Photo: Kevin Todora.

dried herbs, seeds, and bottles of herbal tinctures suggest slivers of these lives and experiences—partial stories that can only be imagined. With *La Charada China*, Lin conjures future transformation. As she builds, she recounts an overlooked story in which unwelcome, oppressive systems are made physical and material, even as she welcomes their dissolution and exorcism.

b. 1973, Houston, TX. Lives and works in Houston

A trio of textile works from **JAMAL CYRUS**'s *Blue Alluvial Glue* series are made from denim, the common workwear material whose dependence on indigo dying implicates it in histories of United States colonial trade, the Middle Passage, and Antebellum southern cotton production. The appearance of these works in St. Louis is also notable, since they function as an homage to the renowned saxophonist and composer Julius Hemphill (1938–1995), who lived here from 1966–73. During this time, Hemphill was instrumental in the founding of the Black Artists Group of St. Louis (BAG), which facilitated collaborations between musicians, actors, dancers, visual artists, educators, and community organizers. His vision of multidisciplinary collaboration resonates with Cyrus, whose own work as an artist and musician bridges visual and sonic realms. Raised in a musical family, he "channels the power of sound as a vehicle for transcendence and identity-building, particularly in relation to Black culture."

Be as a stranger or traveler (Make Me a Pallet on the Floor) (2022) includes a unique piece of textile Cyrus made by gluing together strips of reclaimed denim. With varied washes of denim, this large textile resembles a quilt as well as rows of agricultural plantings, or waves rippling the surface of water. Displayed atop a rammed-earth plinth, this work—like the *Blue Alluvial Glue* series—references the soil deposited by flooding rivers that enriches agricultural lands.

Cyrus insists on continuity and connection between indigo and cotton as agricultural crops harvested by enslaved people often outfitted in hard-wearing denim. He offers a vision of resilience where blues are multivalent—where a rich, natural color is inseparable from a storied Black musical tradition that carries deeply spiritual undertones.

Sonic resonances extend to Cyrus's sculptures that incorporate musical instruments. Though they may be unplayable in the traditional sense, the artist sees them as "opportunities to connect Afro

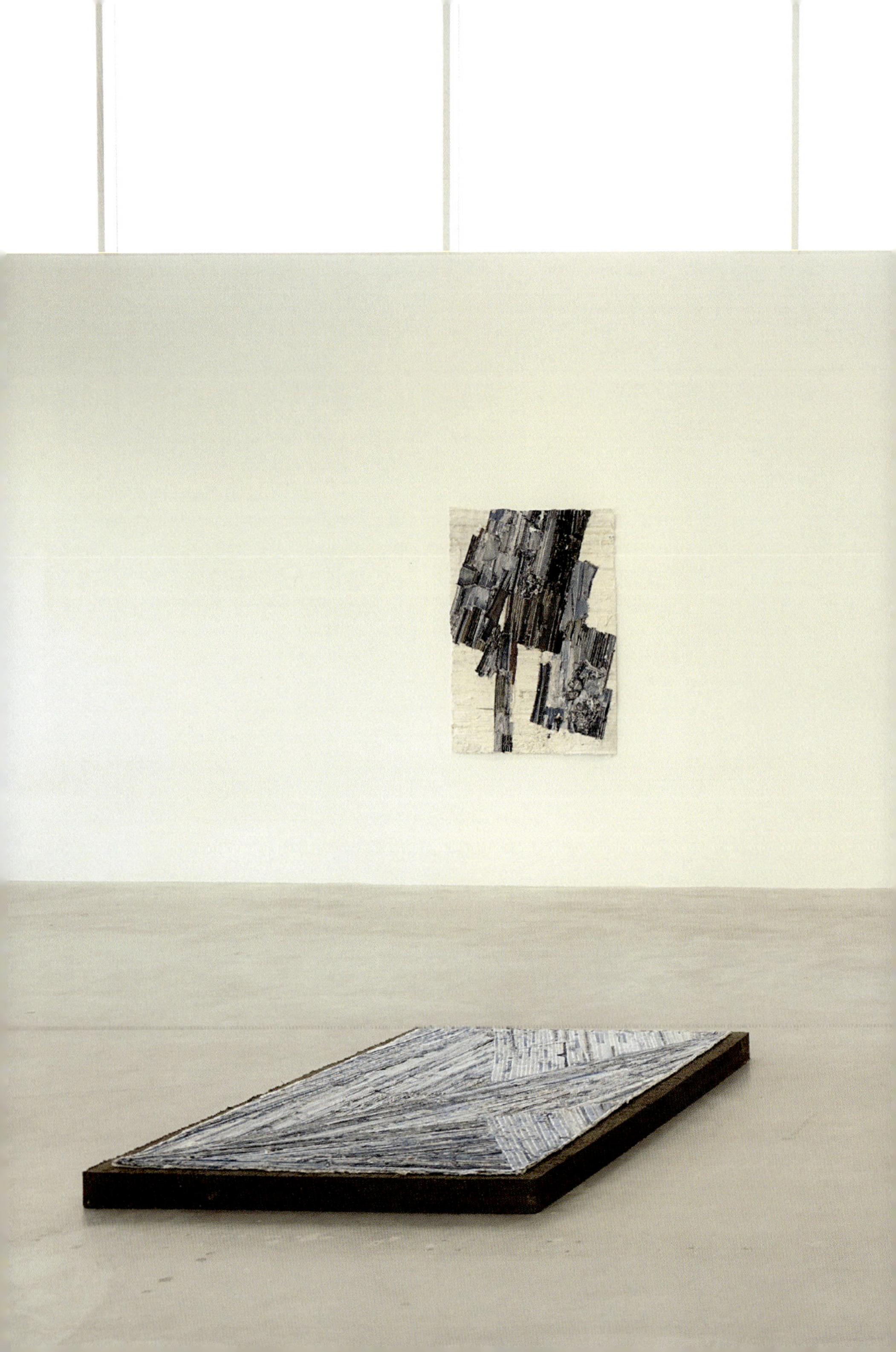

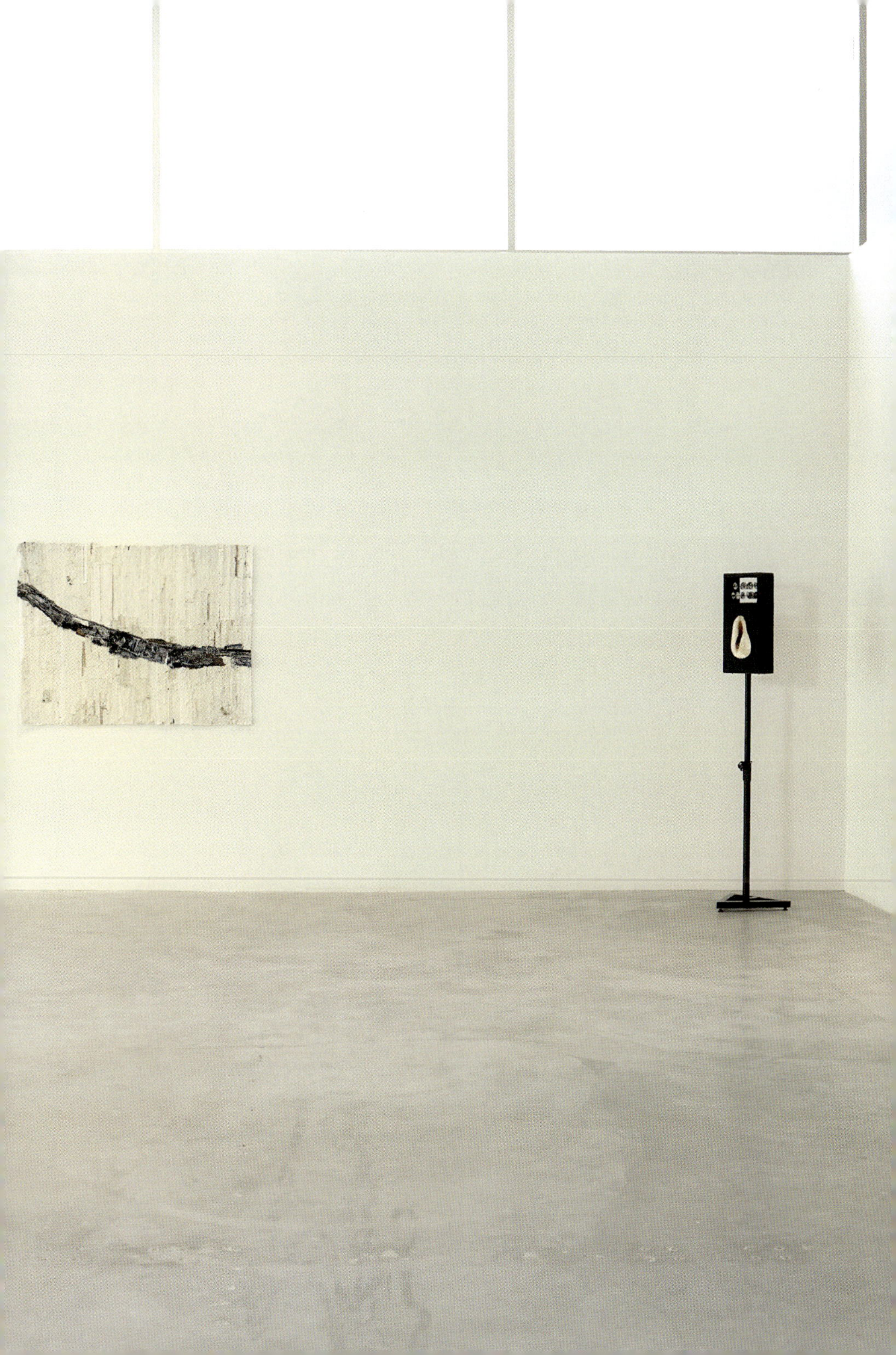

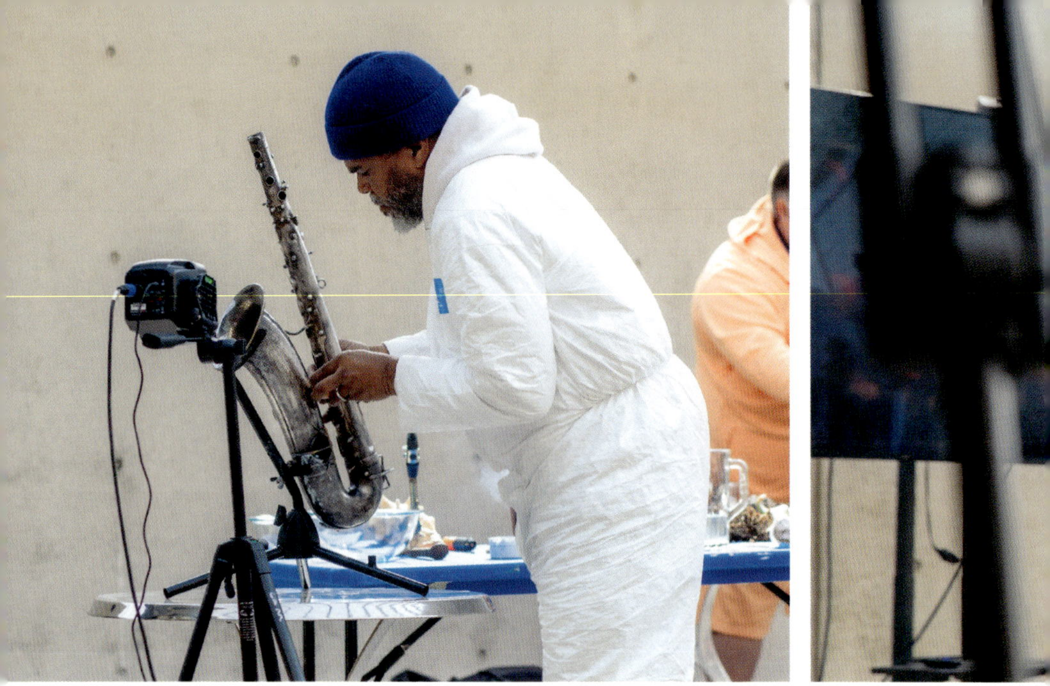

diasporic musical and spiritual traditions." Resembling an ear, the helmet conch shell in Cyrus's sculpture *Sstrum* (2022) seems to be listening in on deeper historical and divine reverberations.

Such connections were viscerally present during Cyrus's *Horn Beam Sacrament*, a performance commissioned for *Like Water* that unfolded in CAM's exterior courtyard. Before an audience of over one hundred people, Cyrus ritually anointed a tenor saxophone. Dressed in white painter's overalls, he washed the saxophone with water collected from the Mississippi River, polished it with Twinkle silver polish, massaged it with aloe, and bathed it in smoke from frankincense, myrrh, and oud. He inserted a railroad spike into its neck, and stuffed its bell with sargassum seaweed. Cyrus wrapped gauze around its body, then covered it with a thick layer of wet, locally-harvested clay. Finally, he placed the prepared saxophone over a live fire in a steel grill the size of a saxophone case covered with a heavy lid, where it smoked for more than twenty-four hours.[1]

While this action unfolded, Cyrus was supported by a group of collaborators whose sonic contributions grounded his seemingly esoteric

Jamal Cyrus, *Horn Beam Sacrament* (performance stills), 2025.

Photos: Tyler Small.

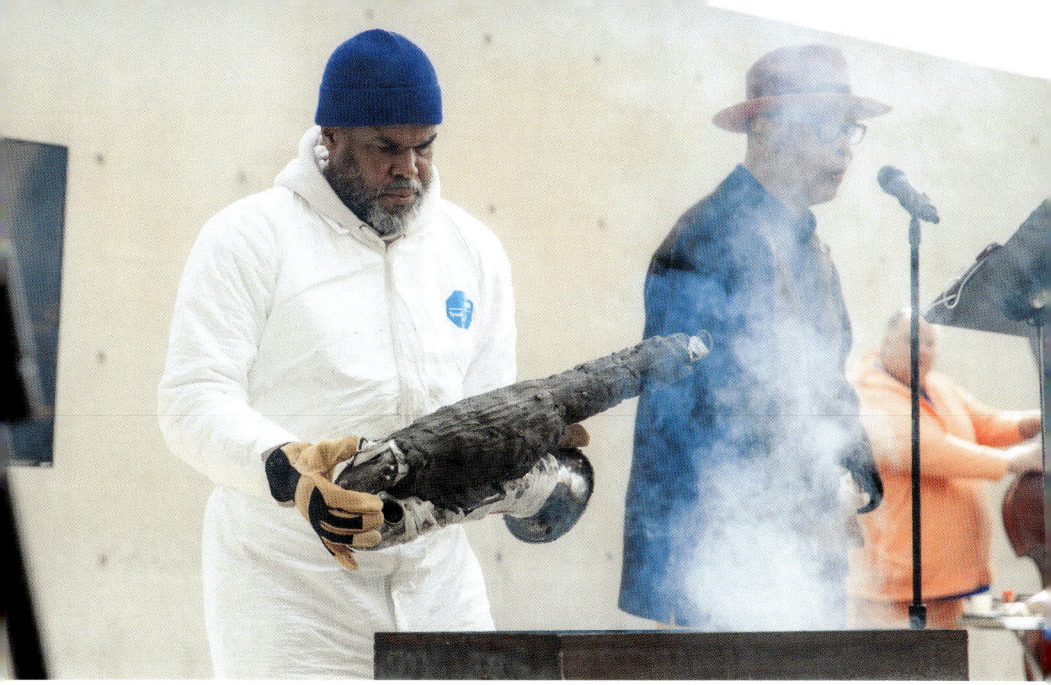

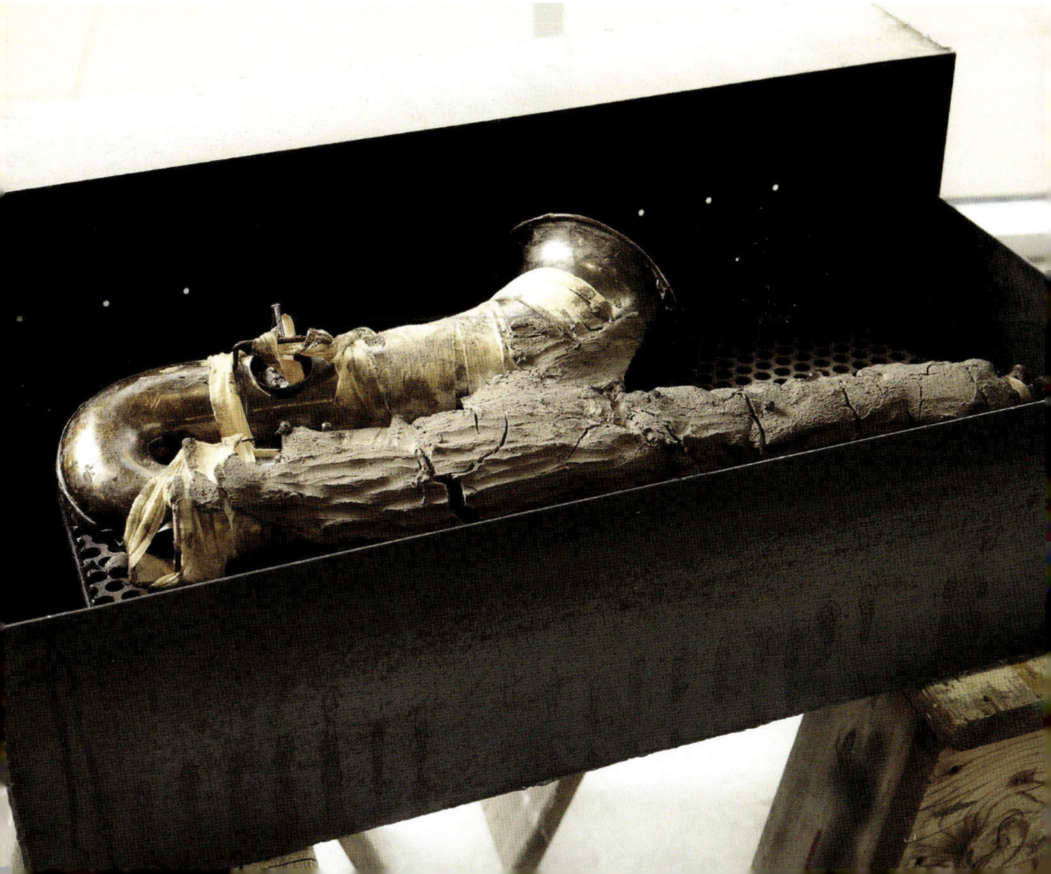

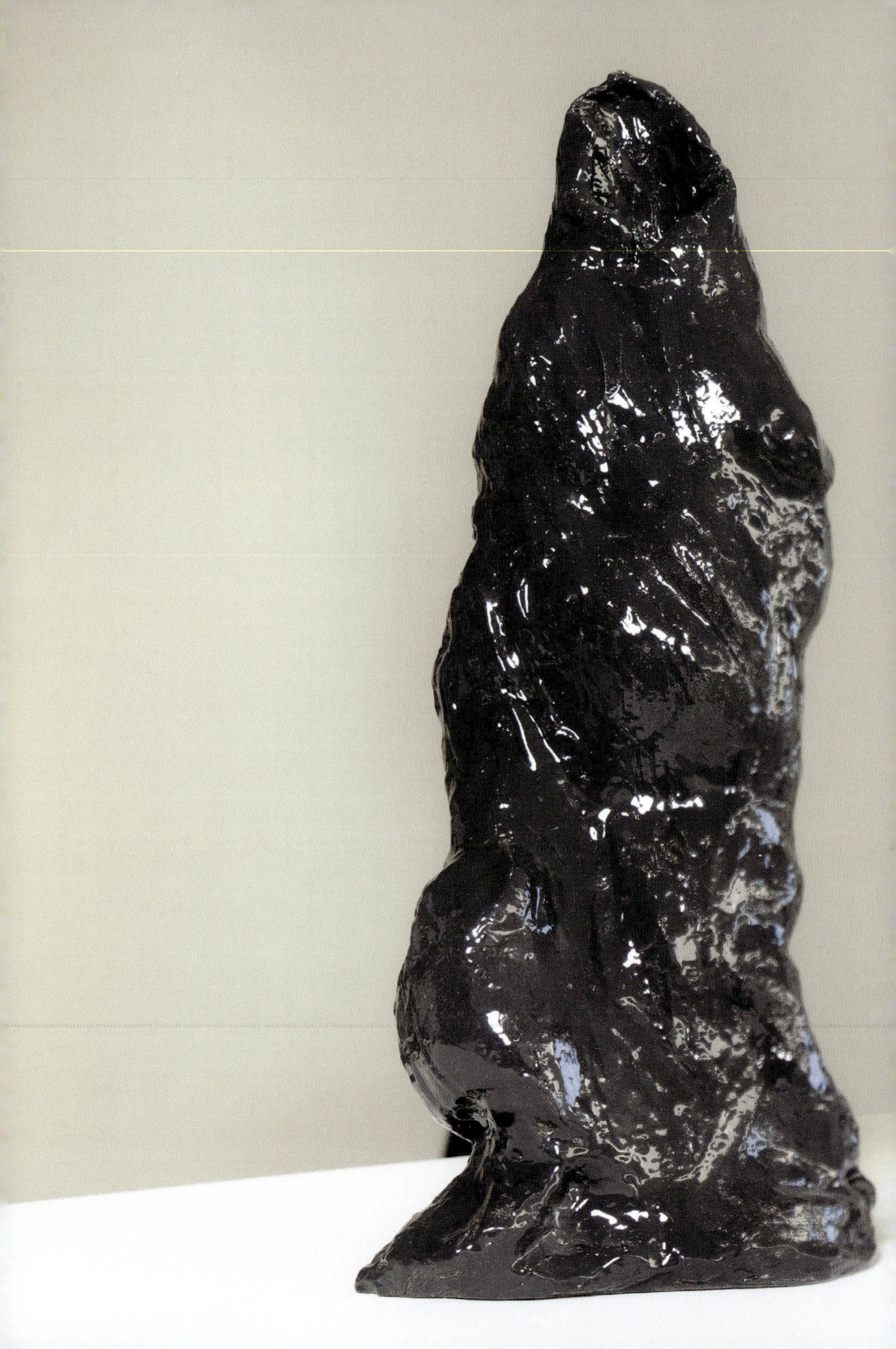

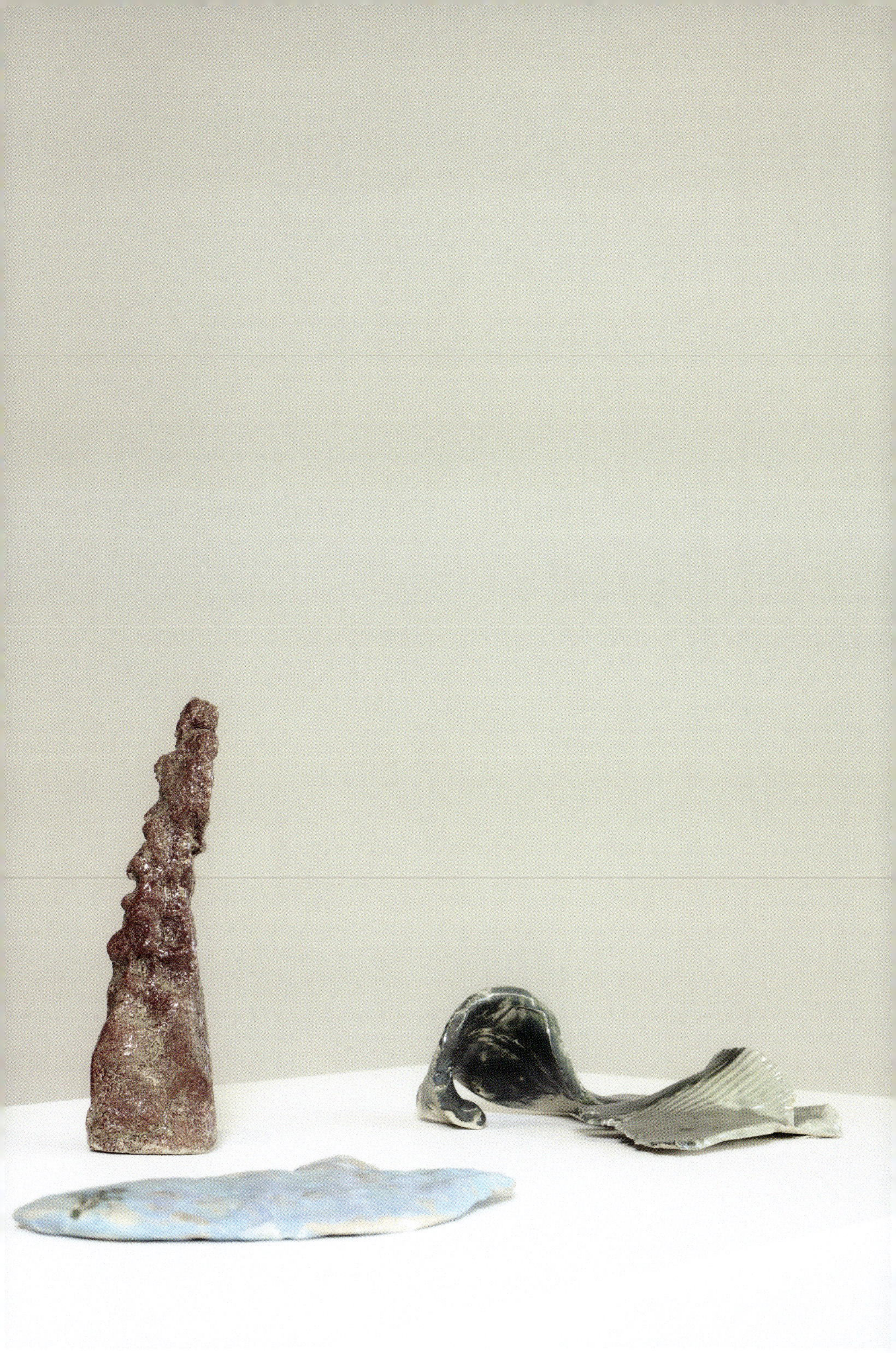

activities and lifted them to new heights. Poet K. Curtis Lyle wrote and recited a poem created for Cyrus that "celebrates the blues as an incorruptible center of our creative reality." Bassist Damon Smith and composer Corey De'Juan Sherrard, Jr. provided scintillating live musical accompaniment throughout the event and played memorable solos. Each performer riffed and responded to all of the others in a seamless, unified orchestration of purpose. As in other works by Cyrus, here, multiple layers also coexist: A recording Lyle made in St. Louis with Julius Hemphill and the vocalist Malinke Kenyatta—*The Collected Poem For Blind Lemon Jefferson* (1971)—was an early inspiration for both *Horn Beam Sacrament* and the *Blue Alluvial Glue* series, making this collaboration a poignant full-circle moment in which Cyrus, Lyle, Sherrard, and Smith's efforts honored local stories while offering new and vital ones.

Temporally-speaking, **SIMONE FATTAL**'s sculptures straddle a position between history and modernity: They appear both ancient—like items one might imagine being unearthed at an archeological dig—and wholly modern, even Modernist. Their lack of fixity makes Fattal's sculpture feel unmoored in time. The forms she imagines in clay include figures, animals, architecture, and even natural phenomena, as in the sculpture *Wave* (2023), whose undulating curves are ridged by dripping ceramic glaze. For Fattal, establishing an unbroken line between the ancient and the modern is wholly intentional. She states: "I am trying to position myself in this line that started with ancient Sumer, and is uninterrupted through today."

b. 1942, Damascus, Syria. Lives and works in Paris, France

Notably, *Like Water* includes a selection of Fattal's earliest ceramic sculptures, which have never before been publicly exhibited. Fattal took refuge in Sausalito, California at the onset of the Lebanese Civil War.[2] While she had previously been a painter, it was in California that Fattal first made ceramic sculptures. One of these—*Goddess of the Springing Water*, made in 1988—was inspired by her memories of an 18th-century BCE Amorite Spring Goddess from the collection of the Aleppo National Museum in Syria, the country of Fattal's birth. The original stone sculpture depicts a woman in a toga-like gown that grazes the ground. She holds a round-bottomed jar with two hands, tilting it away from herself, towards us. In reality, this sculpture, with a hole drilled through its center, would have been placed atop a spring, so that the goddess's jar would continually overflow with water. Fattal's sculpture, though smaller, adopts a similar stance. Her goddess also wears a flowing dress and a stylized headdress, and cradles a small pot in her arms. Fattal incised wavy lines down the front of the figure's gown, drawing in her own suggestion of endlessly flowing water. Occasional bits of stoneware peek out from underneath a light turquoise green glaze, bits of dry earth in an otherwise glassy, wet surface. Fattal's sculpture draws deep into her own well of inspiration as she recalls the original figure by creating one of her own.

Over and over again, we encounter evidence of Fattal's hand and fingers. We can imagine her tracing and shaping damp clay by following the trails her fingertips made while wiping across or gouging into wet surfaces. We can see the delicate cracks that form as Fattal coaxes a drying slab of clay into a curve.

As humans created images of their gods, so too did many believe that gods created humankind by sculpting us from mud. In *Fix Your Gaze on Saturn's Rings* (2012–2022), the artist's expressive manual gestures are frozen permanently in a bronze sculpture of a seated figure who seems pinched together like one of these mythological figures.

Likewise do Fattal's collaged-paper works showcase the artist freely mixing historical and contemporary registers. In *Le Grand Renversement 1948* [The Great Reversal 1948] (2012), viewers encounter a broad range of cut-out images—from utilitarian objects like bowls and vases, to images of works by other artists, animal and human figurines, snapshots of a whale's tail, Arabic calligraphy recalling the names of cities, and architectural structures. These cutouts float atop and beside each other, glued to the surface of a singular image that depicts delicate waves rippling the surface of a body of water, and throwing off spectral reflections. Fattal's work reminds us that we are time's subjects, and that inspiration is not subjected to the constraints of time.

b. 1988, New York City, NY. Lives and works in Columbus, OH

DIONNE LEE's photographs and videos establish connections between water, the natural world, drawing, and time. Across the three black-and-white gelatin silver prints in her series *Rock Drawing III* (20"24), we see a spiral the artist has painted onto a rock with water, as she photographs its changing states. Over the series, the water is pulled into or

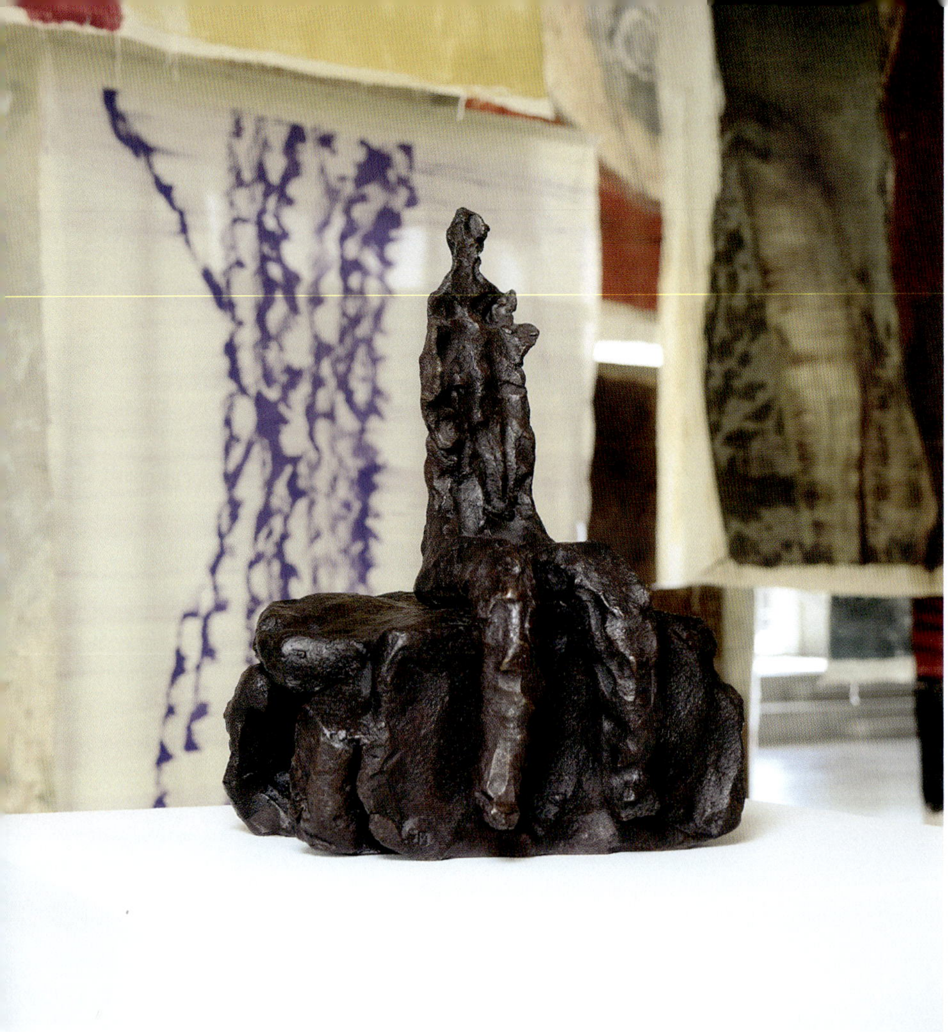

Simone Fattal, *Fix Your Gaze On Saturn's Rings*, 2012–2022. Bronze, 25 1/2 × 19 11/16 × 15 3/4 inches.

Courtesy the artist and kaufmann repetto, Milan and New York. Photo: Izaiah Johnson.

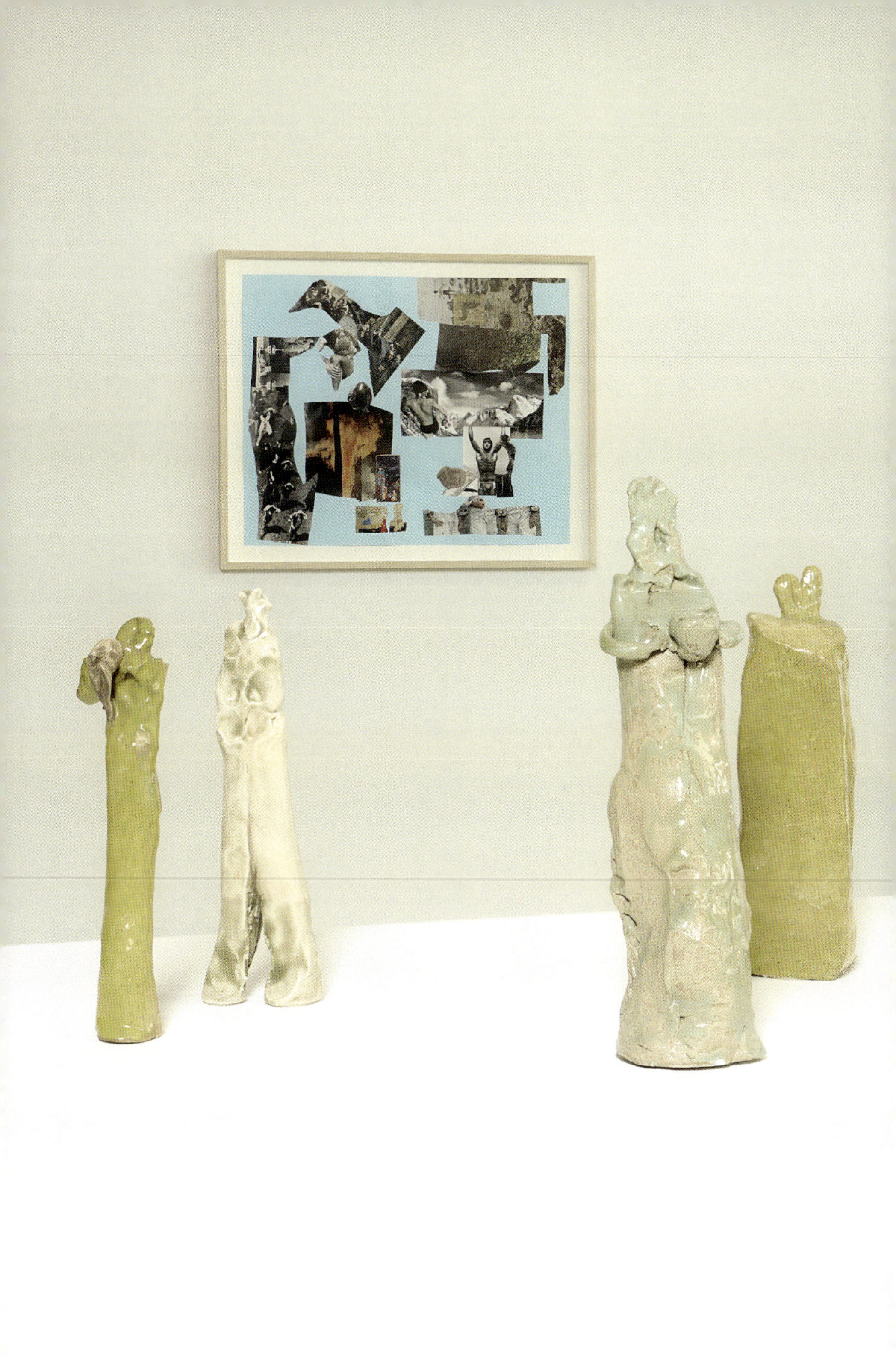

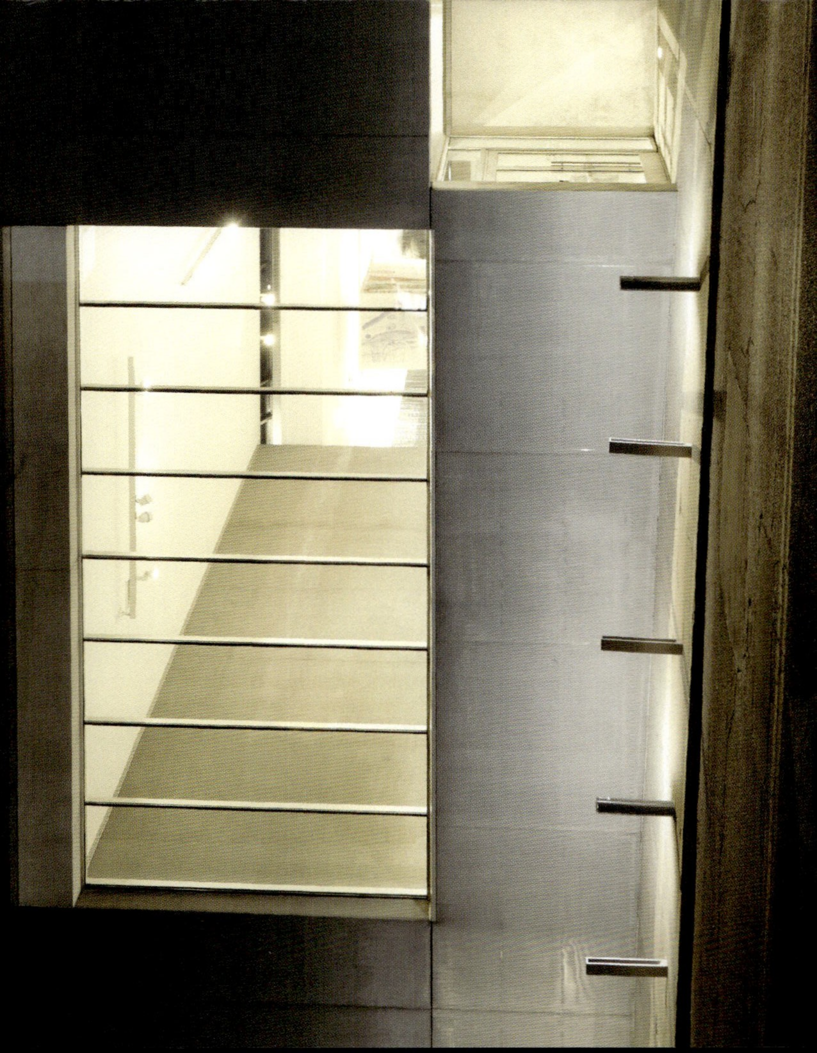

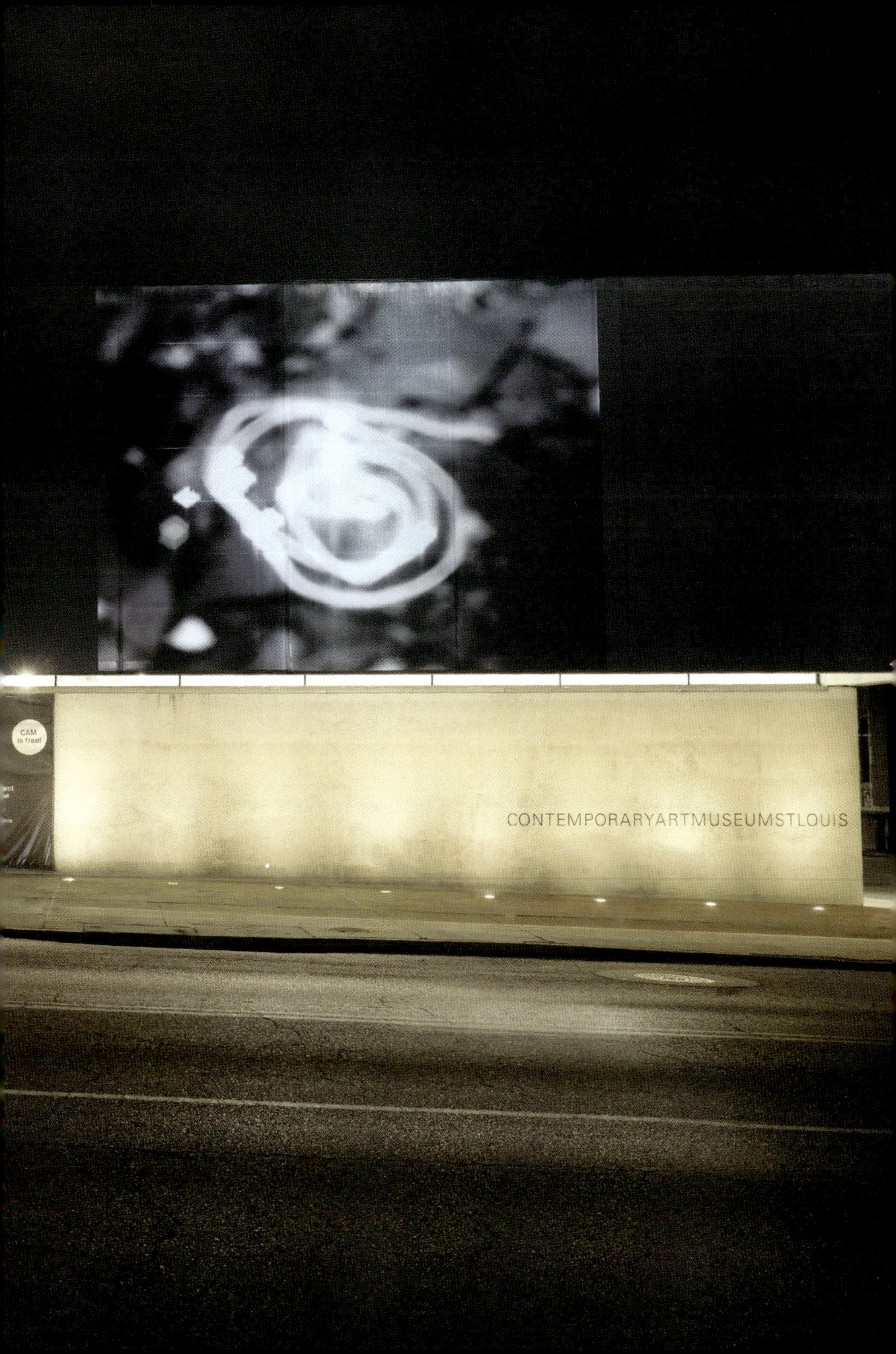
CAM
is free!
CONTEMPORARYARTMUSEUMSTLOUIS

evaporates from the rock. The spiral itself—symbolizing both cyclicality and revolution—offers metaphors of accumulation and dissolution, backward and forward motion, interiority and expansiveness.

In and out of the darkroom, Lee engages with photography's materiality. In an age when many image makers print digitally, Lee remains committed to analog darkroom processes. For the earliest print in this exhibition, *Breaking Wave* (2018), Lee photographed and printed a black-and-white image of a swelling ocean wave. Later, she tore this print in two and photographed the pieces held in her hands in front of a black fabric backdrop. Like a two-piece puzzle, the image may be splitting apart or coming together. Either way, Lee has fixed this moment in time, even while she demonstrates how her engagement with analog photography can stretch her medium's temporal reach.

Lee's dedicatedly physical approach to her medium is also apparent in *Untitled Rock Drawing VI* (2024). To make this solarized silver gelatin print, Lee exposed photographic paper to light through a negative. As the image begins to develop, Lee stills the process by exposing the print to a short burst of light—typically something that most photographers would fastidiously avoid. This process partially inverts the tonality of the image, making some light areas appear dark. Here again, we encounter a spiral in the form of a coiled rope that draws our attention inward. Knots running the length of the the pictured rope establish an elemental rhythm—small interruptions along a hypnotic path.

Furling and unfurling spirals appear in Lee's videos *Currents* and *Untitled* (both 2024). Shooting with a handheld camera, Lee follows a coiled piece of rope as it floated down a stream. On its meandering journey, the rope eventually encountered resistance that caused it to unwind like a living line drawing.[3] In *Untitled*, Lee's video camera auto-focused on the motion of light dancing on the surface of the water, rather than the spiraling rope, which remains out of focus in the video's background. Lee's camera saw the reflections as triangular packets of light that resemble shooting stars. As her work often does, this video connects microcosmic and macrocosmic views of the world around us.

Diving further into photography's orchestration of light and timing, both Lee's photograph *Untitled* (2023) and her video *Walking*

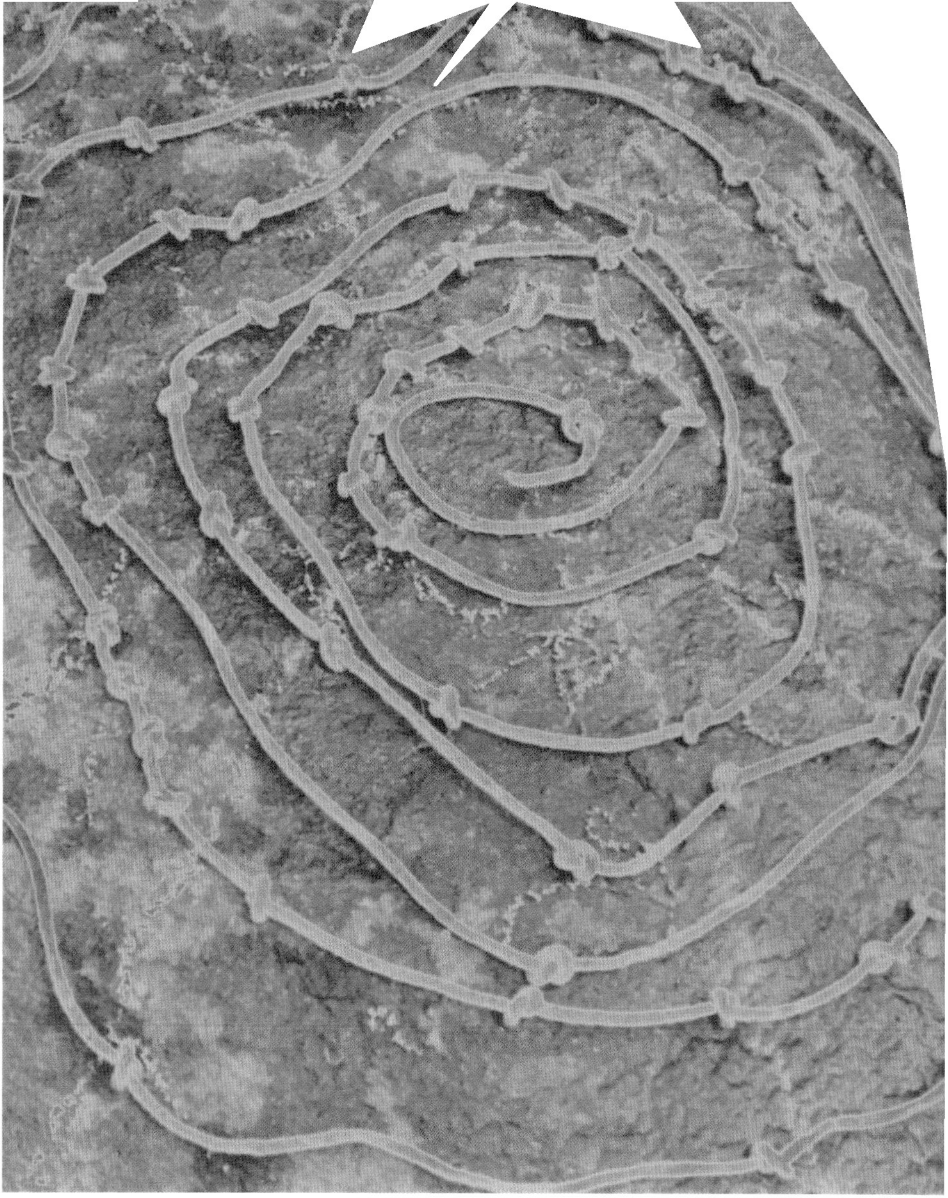

Dionne Lee, *Untitled Rock Drawing VI,* 2024. Solarized gelatin silver print, 10 × 8 inches.

Courtesy the artist and P.Bibeau, New York.

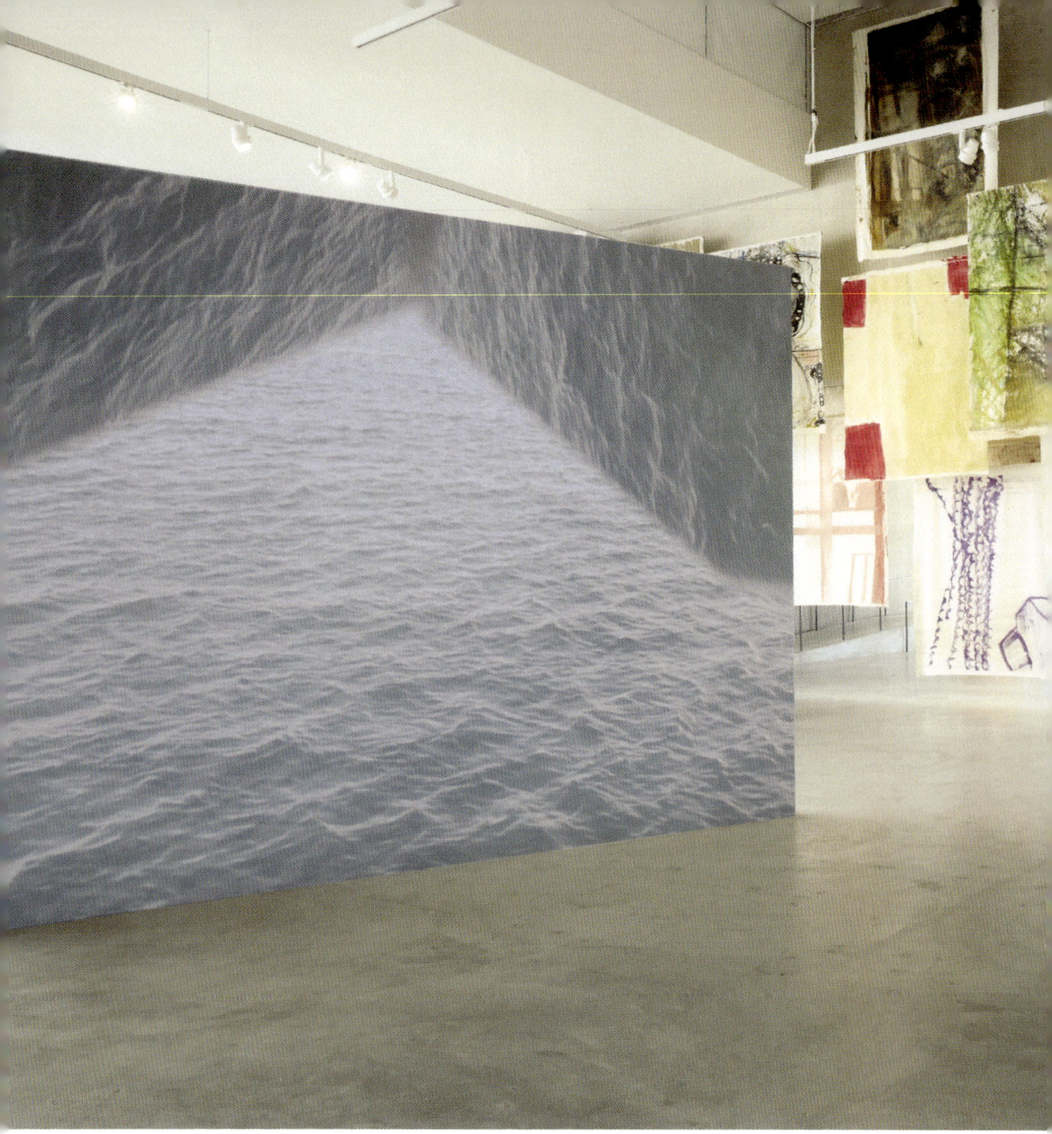

Beatriz Santiago Muñoz, *Otros usos* [Other Uses] (still), 2014. Installation view, *Like Water*, Contemporary Art Museum St. Louis, March 7–August 10, 2025.

Photo: Izaiah Johnson.

Stick IV (2024) incorporate divining rods—the forked sticks traditionally used to locate underground sources of water. Here, branching forms resemble the hands of a ticking clock. Both of these works also offer viewers an opportunity to consider the invisible underground currents Lee is connecting with, histories and moments unseen, underground, in darkness.

b. 1972, San Juan, Puerto Rico. Lives and works in San Juan

BEATRIZ SANTIAGO MUÑOZ's single-channel video *Otros usos* [Other Uses] (2014) offers an interpretation of a fractured history. To create it, Santiago Muñoz fabricated a mirrored housing for her film camera, effectively turning it into a kaleidoscope of sorts. Shot on and around a pier at a former United States military base in Ceiba, Puerto Rico, Santiago Muñoz captures images of the sea, local fisherman, the pier itself, and abandoned Naval property and infrastructure. Projected on a large wall, *Otros usos*'s formal qualities create a fascinating—if occasionally disorienting—marine portal. We're used to seeing the ocean recede in flatness towards the horizon, so when Santiago Muñoz turns this image on its head or side, it becomes difficult to understand which end is up so to speak. Water feels as though it could spill out of the filmic frame. Conceptually, the film poetically amplifies the complex and fragmented political relationship between the mainland United States and this Caribbean territory.[4] *Otros usos* calls to mind rising sea levels and the ecological challenges wrought by tropical storms as a result of our world's rapidly shifting climate and rising sea levels.

Pájaro, cómeme (Filoctetes) [Bird, Eat Me (Philoctetes)] (2023) is another work by Santiago Muñoz that digs into the complex, colonial relationship between the mainland United States and Puerto Rico. This multi-channel installation unfolds across three screens in a darkened room. Shot on film and transferred to video, *Pájaro cómeme* retains the graininess and saturated color of analog film stock. For this work, the artist recounts the myth of Philoctetes, a famed Greek archer who was bitten on the foot by a snake as he traveled to wage war in Troy. Suffering from an infected wound, as Philoctetes cried out in pain, his fellow soldiers grew increasingly disturbed; they left him stranded on the island of Lemnos when they sailed on to war. For her filmic adaptation, Santiago Muñoz cast a friend—rather than a professional actor—to play the mythical warrior. Her approach, which

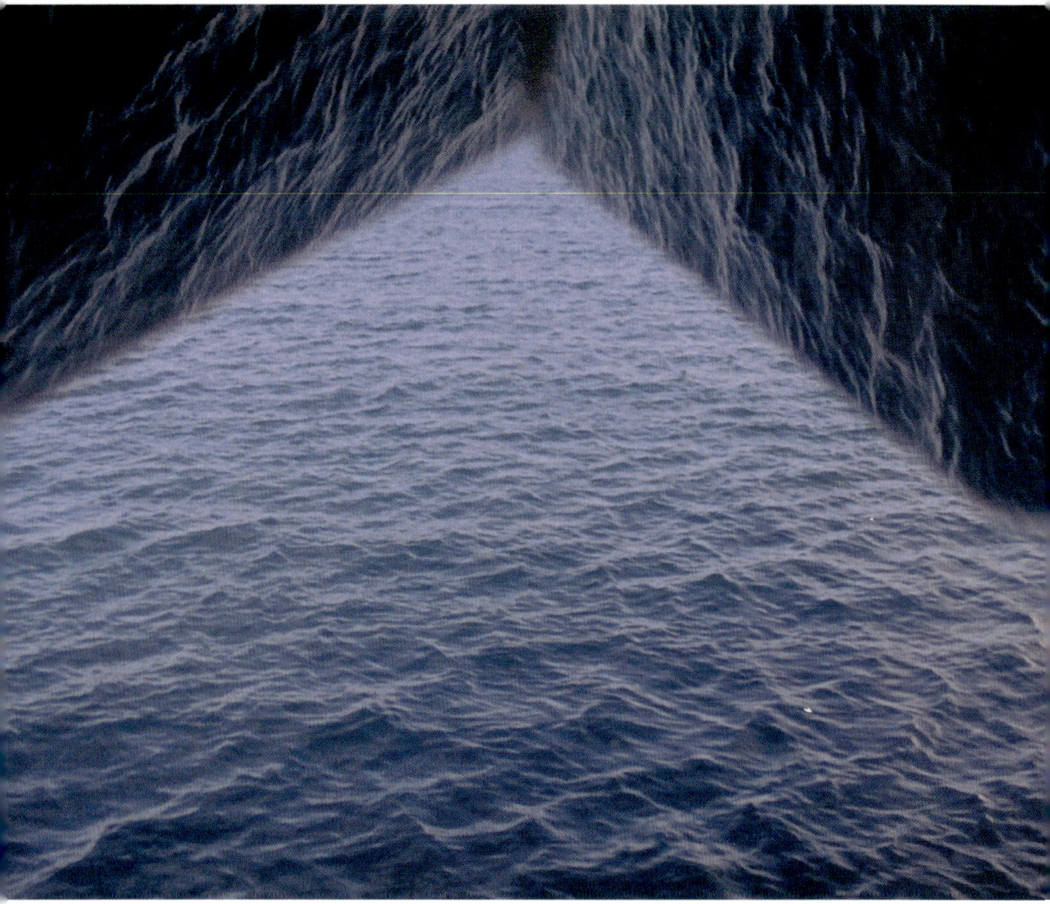

Beatriz Santiago Muñoz, *Otros usos* [Otros Usos] (still), 2014. Single-channel video (color, sound), 6:52 minutes.

Courtesy the artist and Sociedad del Tiempo Libre, San Juan, Puerto Rico.

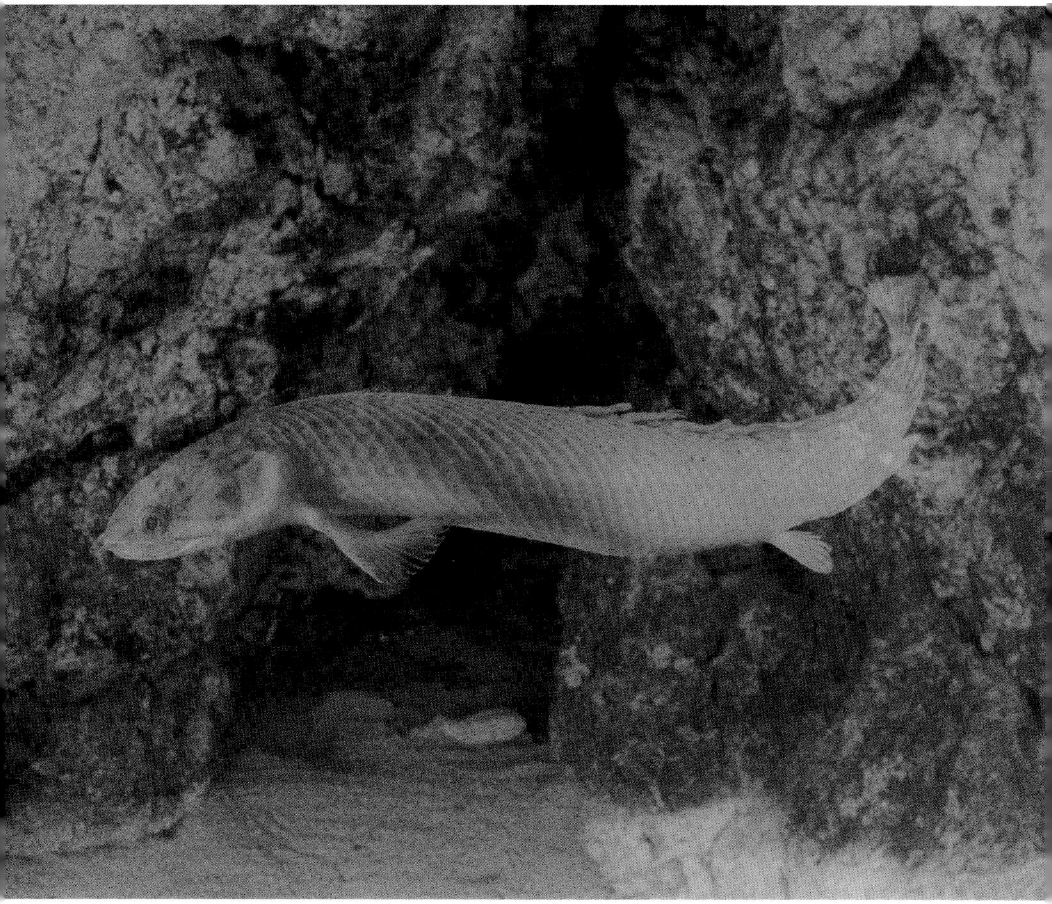

Beatriz Santiago Muñoz, *Pájaro, cómeme (Filoctetes)* [Bird, Eat Me (Philoctetes)] (still), 2023. Three-channel video (black and white and color, sound), 6:44 minutes.

Courtesy the artist and Sociedad del Tiempo Libre, San Juan, Puerto Rico.

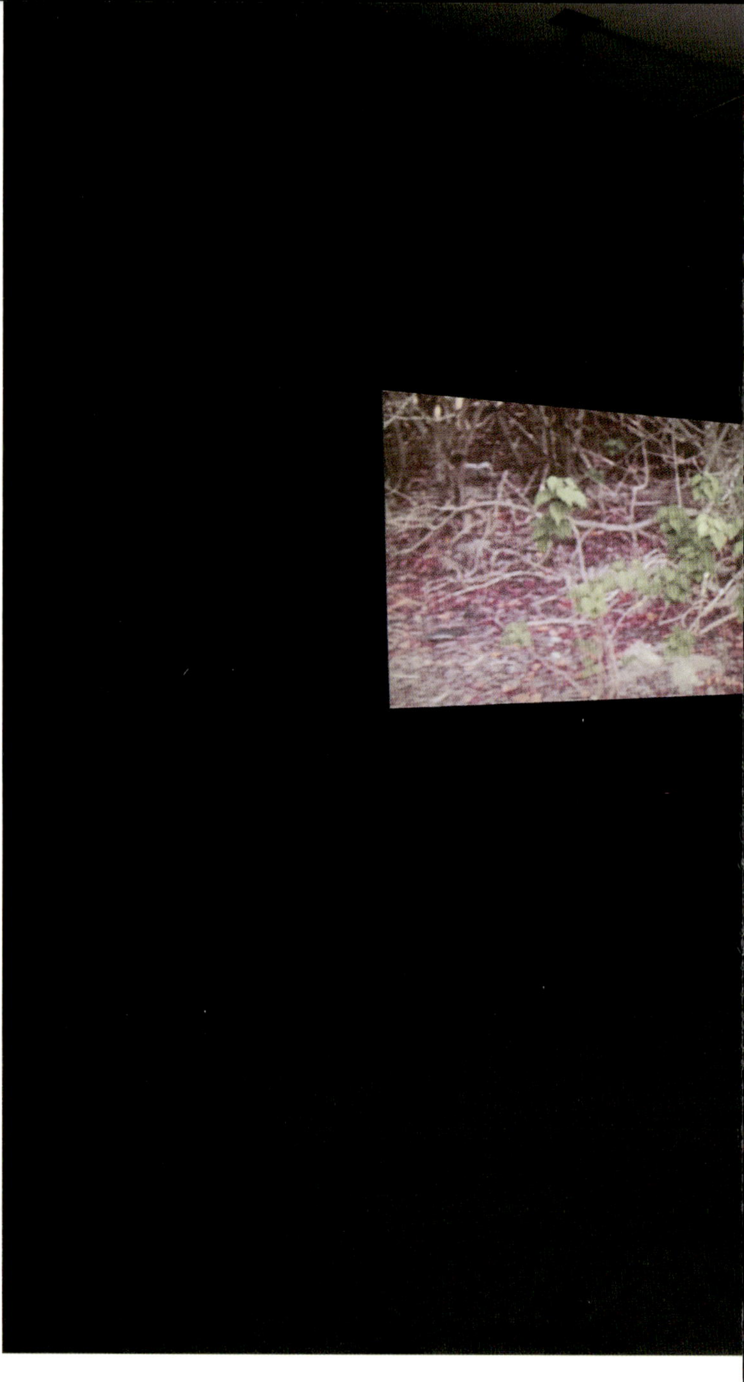

Beatriz Santiago Muñoz, *Pájaro, cómeme (Filoctetes)* [Bird, Eat Me (Philoctetes)], 2023. Installation view, *Like Water*, Contemporary Art Museum St. Louis, March 7–August 10, 2025.

Photo: Izaiah Johnson.

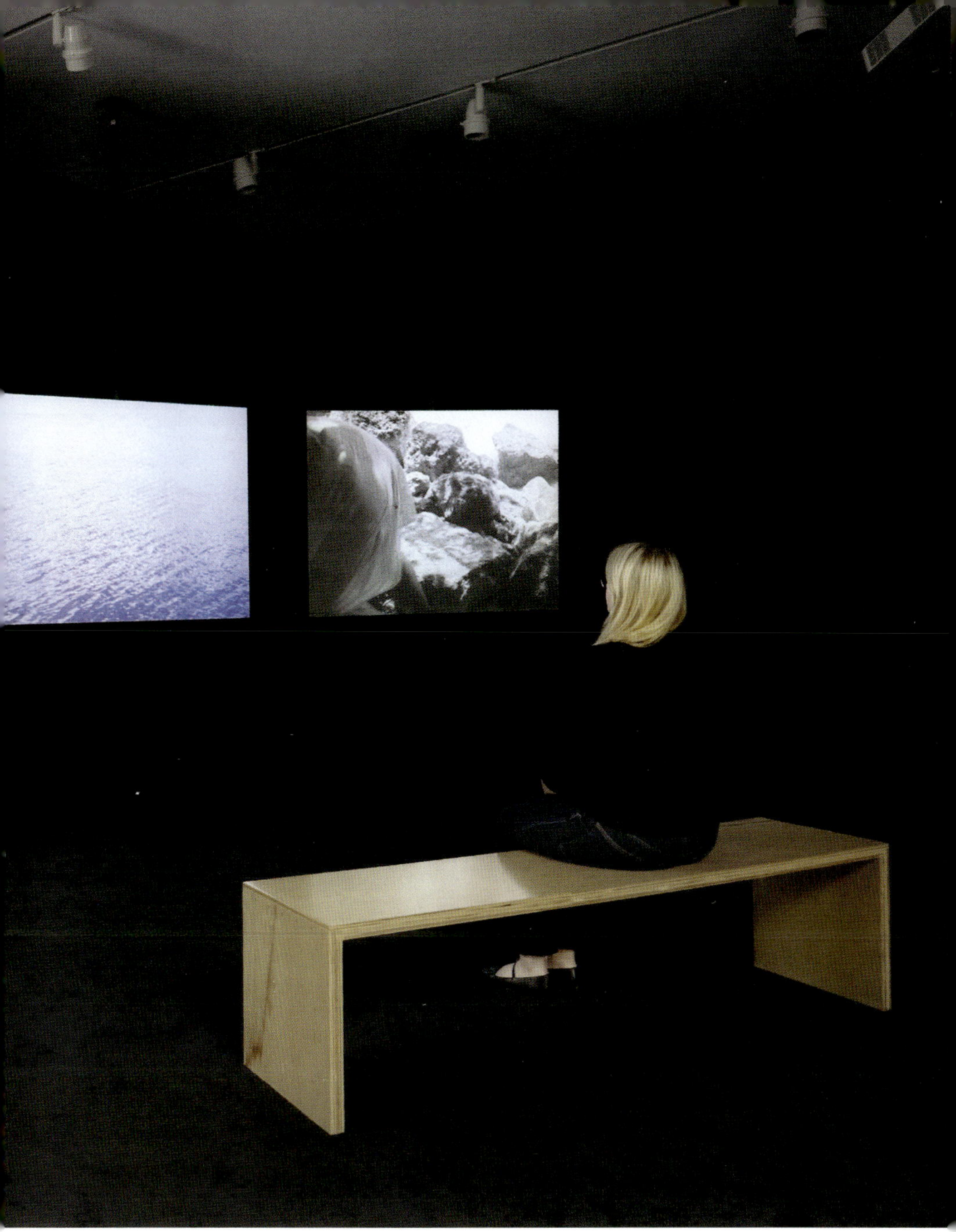

she calls the "sensory unconscious," is also decidedly less narrative. Across color and black-and-white moving images, we see caves, Classical statuary, bows and arrows, a contemporary man relaxing in a hammock, and a figure limping along a beachfront in a toga, attending to a wounded foot. Santiago Muñoz draws salient parallels between Philoctetes's abandonment on Lemnos and Puerto Rico's left-behind status by the mainland United States, especially as seen in light of the island's economic challenges following damage by recent hurricanes, flooding, and catastrophic weather events.

VIVIAN SUTER's gestural use of acrylic paint may be the most immediate way that her work evokes fluidity, but it is just one of many. Suter lives and paints in outdoor studios on a former coffee plantation in Panajachel, Guatemala. Here in a high altitude jungle, her work is subject to rain, humidity, and unpredictable weather events—she has, for instance, dug paintings out of the muck following a mudslide. In other cases, leaves may blow across and stick to wet painted surfaces.

b. 1949, Buenos Aires, Argentina. Lives and works in Panajachel, Guatemala

Suter's paintings further suggest fluidity as she slides between abstract and representative modes. Some of her paintings evoke botanical specimens including trees, leaves, vines, and unfurling sprouts. We might also notice outlines suggesting Suter's dogs—the beloved Tintin, Bonzo, Nina, and Disco—or even, on occasion, pawprints they've tracked over drying canvases. Yet many other images hover at the edges of legibility, suggesting waning shadows on walls or architectural gridlines. And in some paintings, it is clear that Suter is playing experimentally with color, structure, transparency, and line. We see her recording the swing of her arms through broad, sweeping gestures, the ways paint soaks into raw cotton, or how it drips or blends into other colors.

Across a display that includes more than eighty paintings, it becomes clear that Suter is not content with a signature or singular approach to her medium or craft. Freedom, it seems, is her modus operandi. Uniquely among painters, Suter does not title or date her canvases; instead, her paintings speak for themselves and harmonize with each other. And Suter's spatial strategy differentiates her from artists for whom painting is a distinctly two-dimensional affair. Her signature dense arrangements of canvases straddle a line between

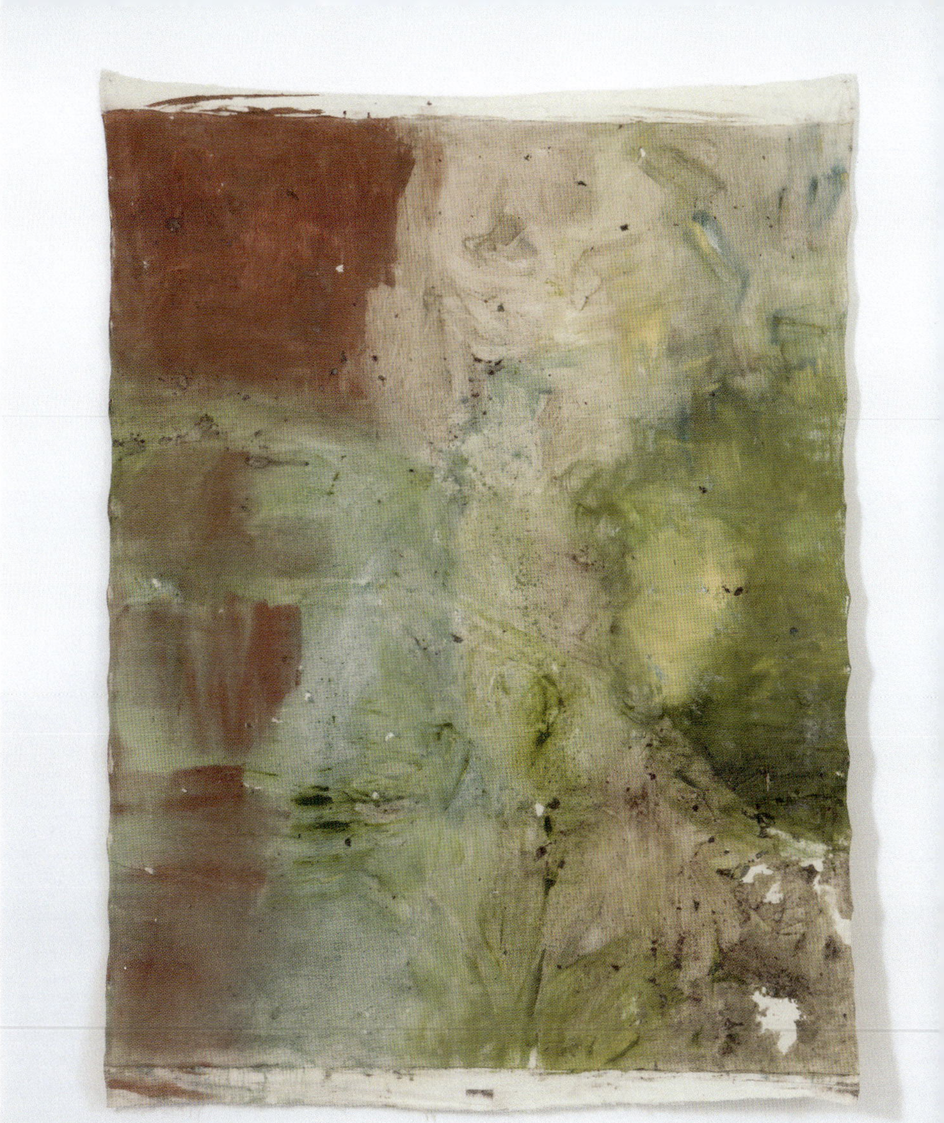

Vivian Suter, No title, n.d. Mixed media on canvas, 94 3⁄4 × 70 7⁄8 inches. © Vivian Suter.

Courtesy the artist and Gladstone Gallery, New York. Photo: David Regen.

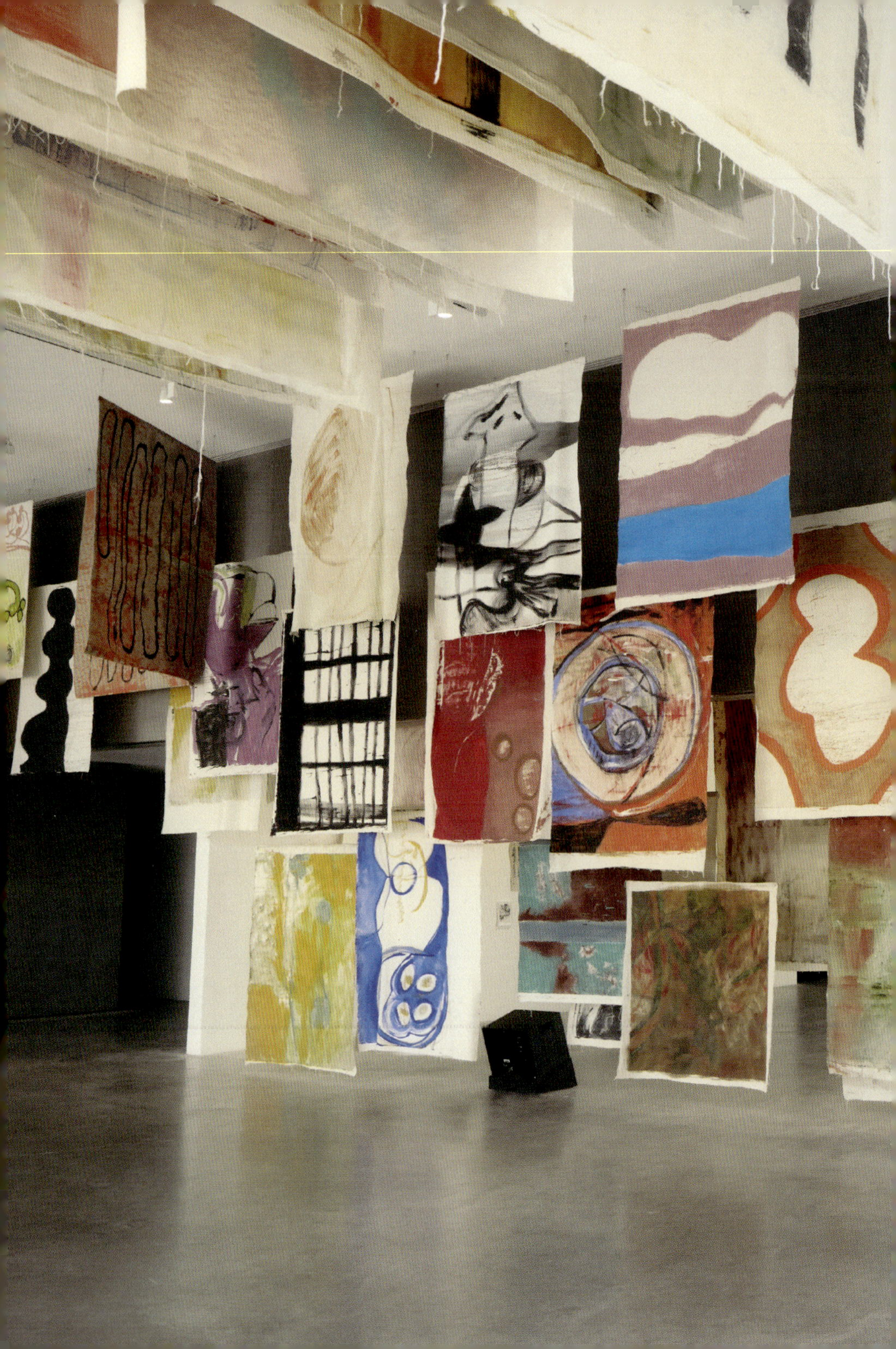

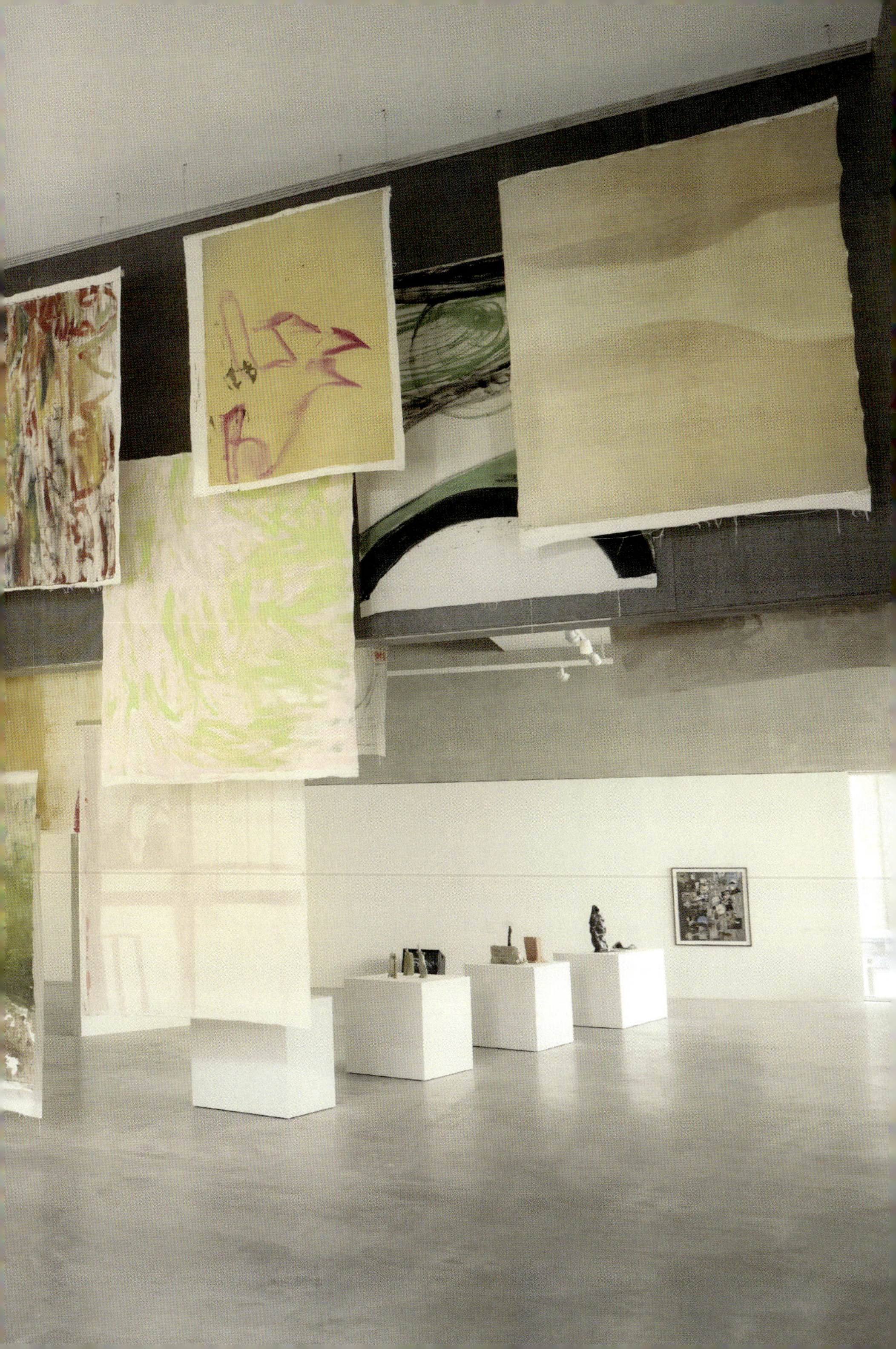

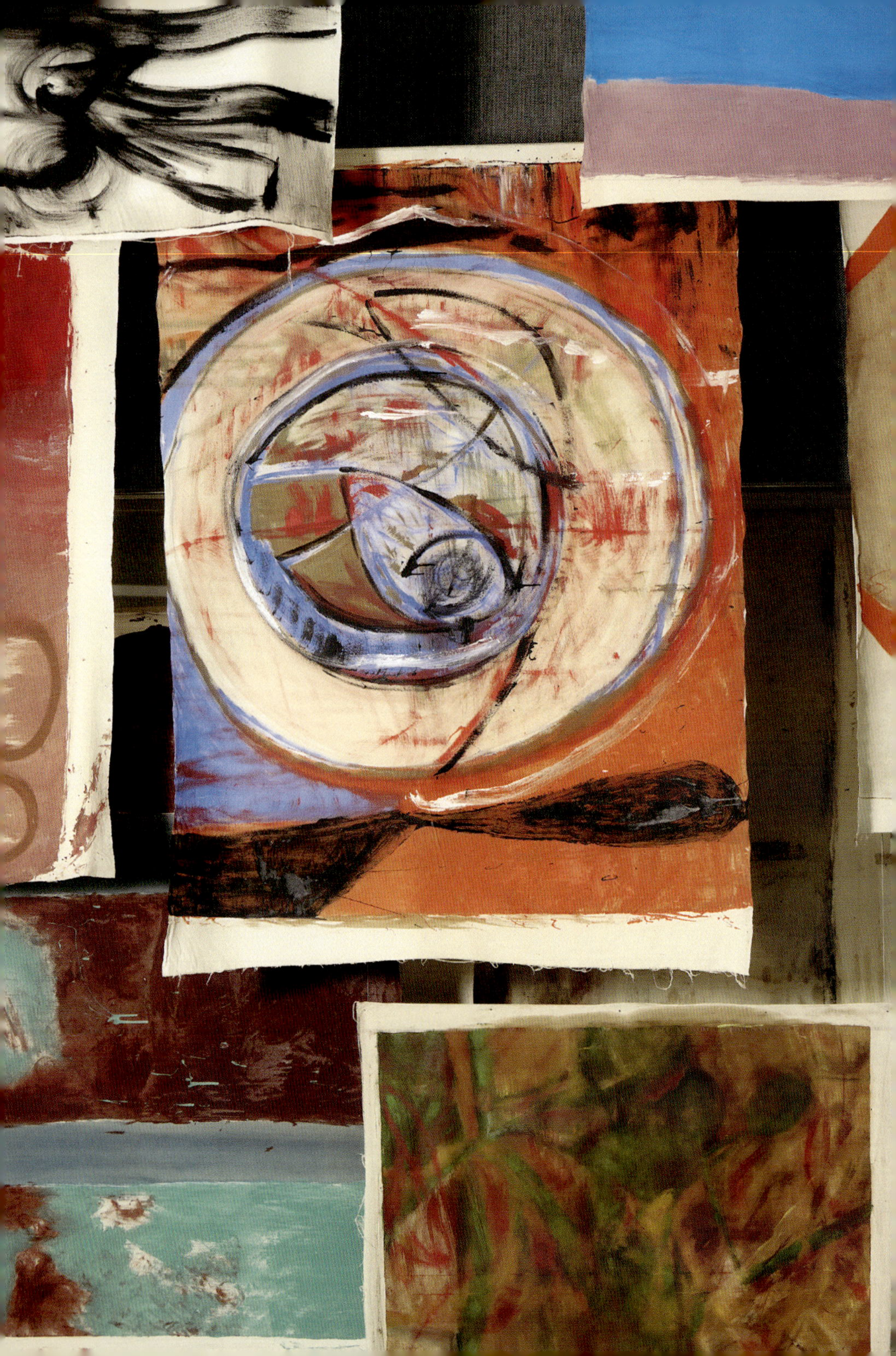

elegance and riotousness, creating immersive architectures all their own. We flow through and around them, never taking them in at a single glance. With an approach that is both decisively punk and respectful of her medium's material, spatial, and conceptual possibilities, Suter charts a new course for her work.

NOTES

1. After it cooled outdoors, Cyrus's prepared saxophone was exhibited in the gallery.

2. It was in California that Fattal started Post-Apollo Press, an adventurous imprint that published important works of poetry, prose, and translations for more than thirty years.

3. Dionne Lee's video *Untitled* was projected on CAM's façade every evening from dusk to midnight as part of CAM's Street Views program.

4. While Puerto Ricans are considered US citizens, they lack political representation: Puerto Ricans cannot vote in US Presidential elections and do not have voting representation in Congress.

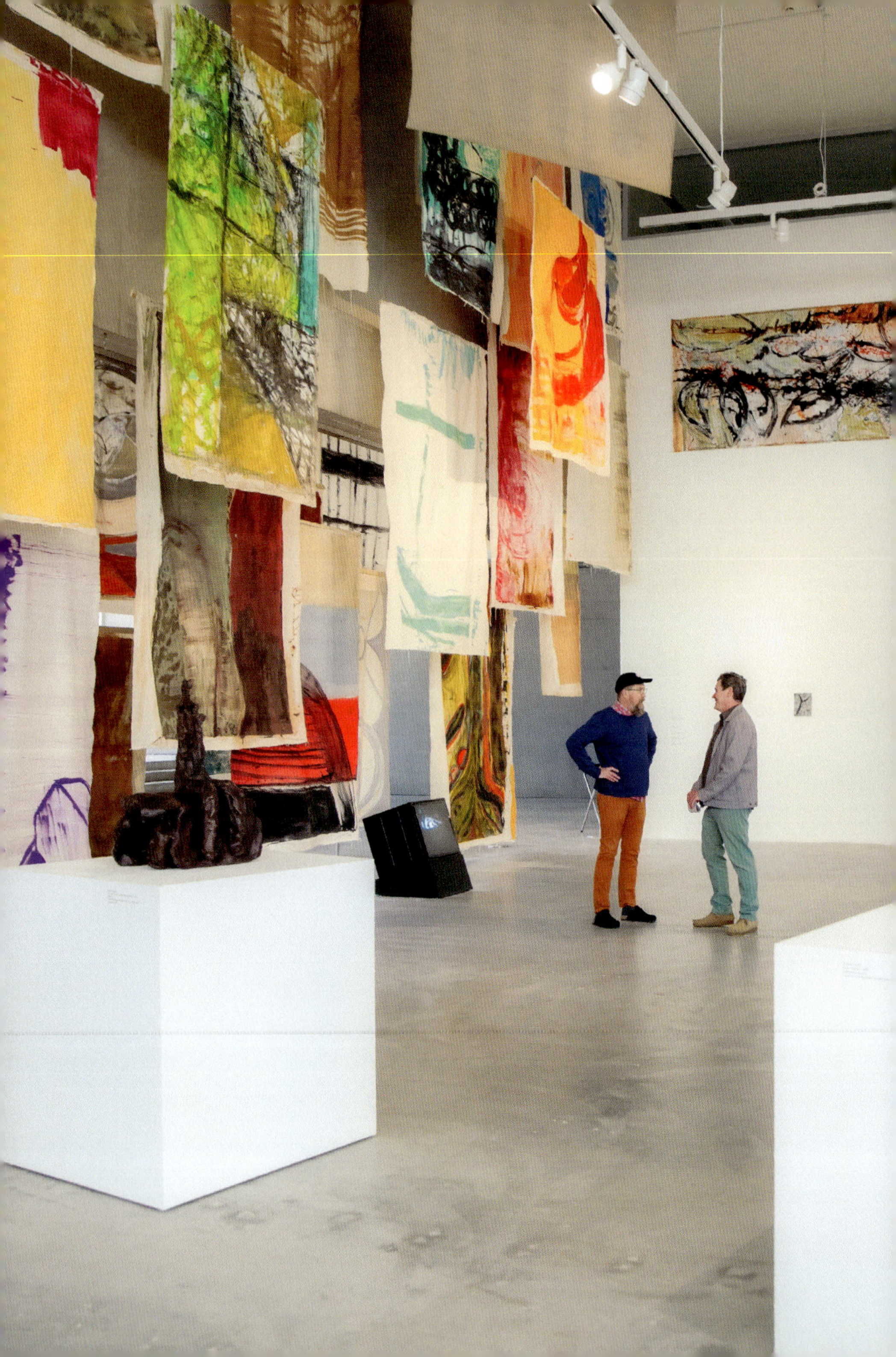

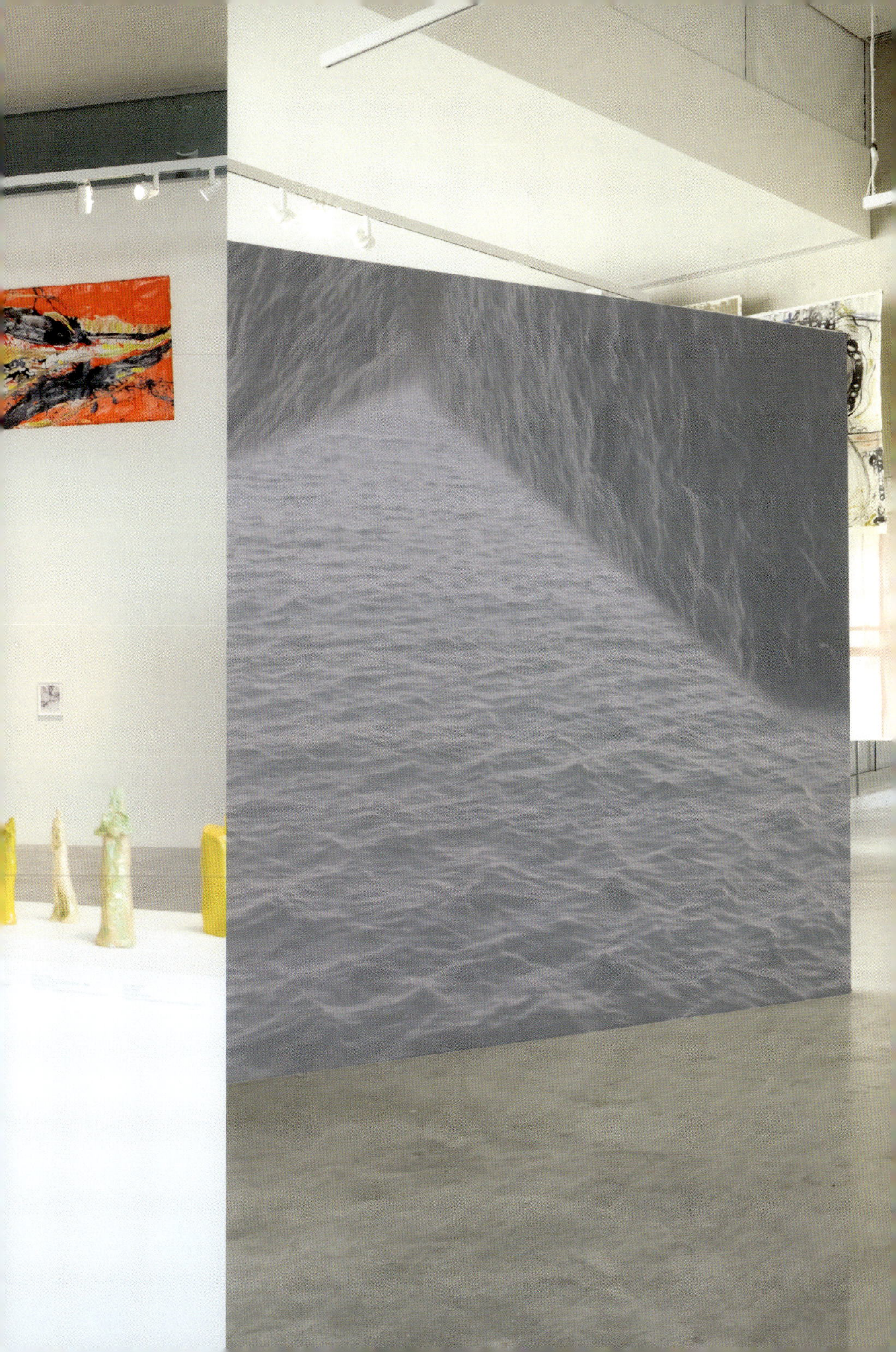

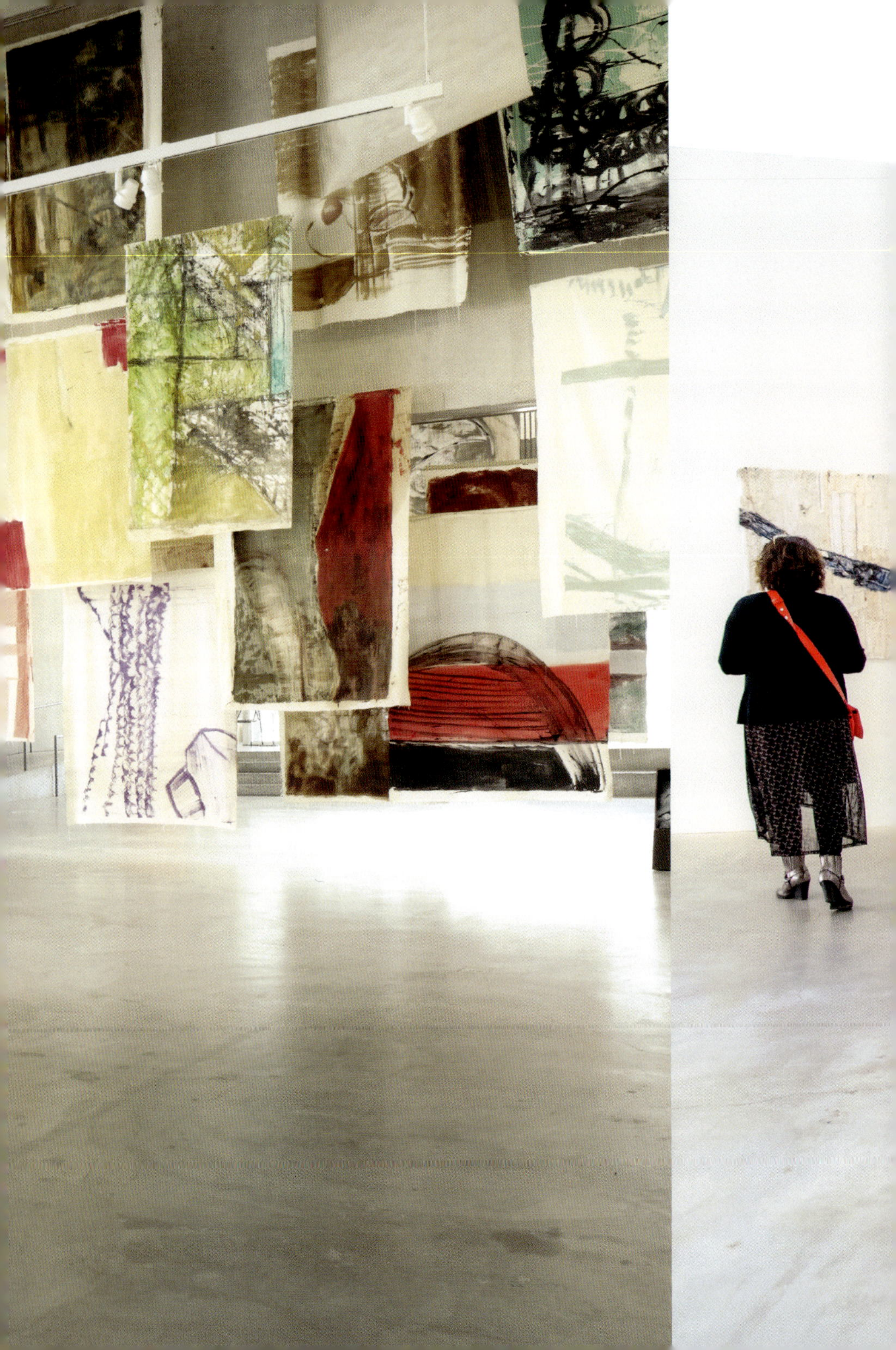

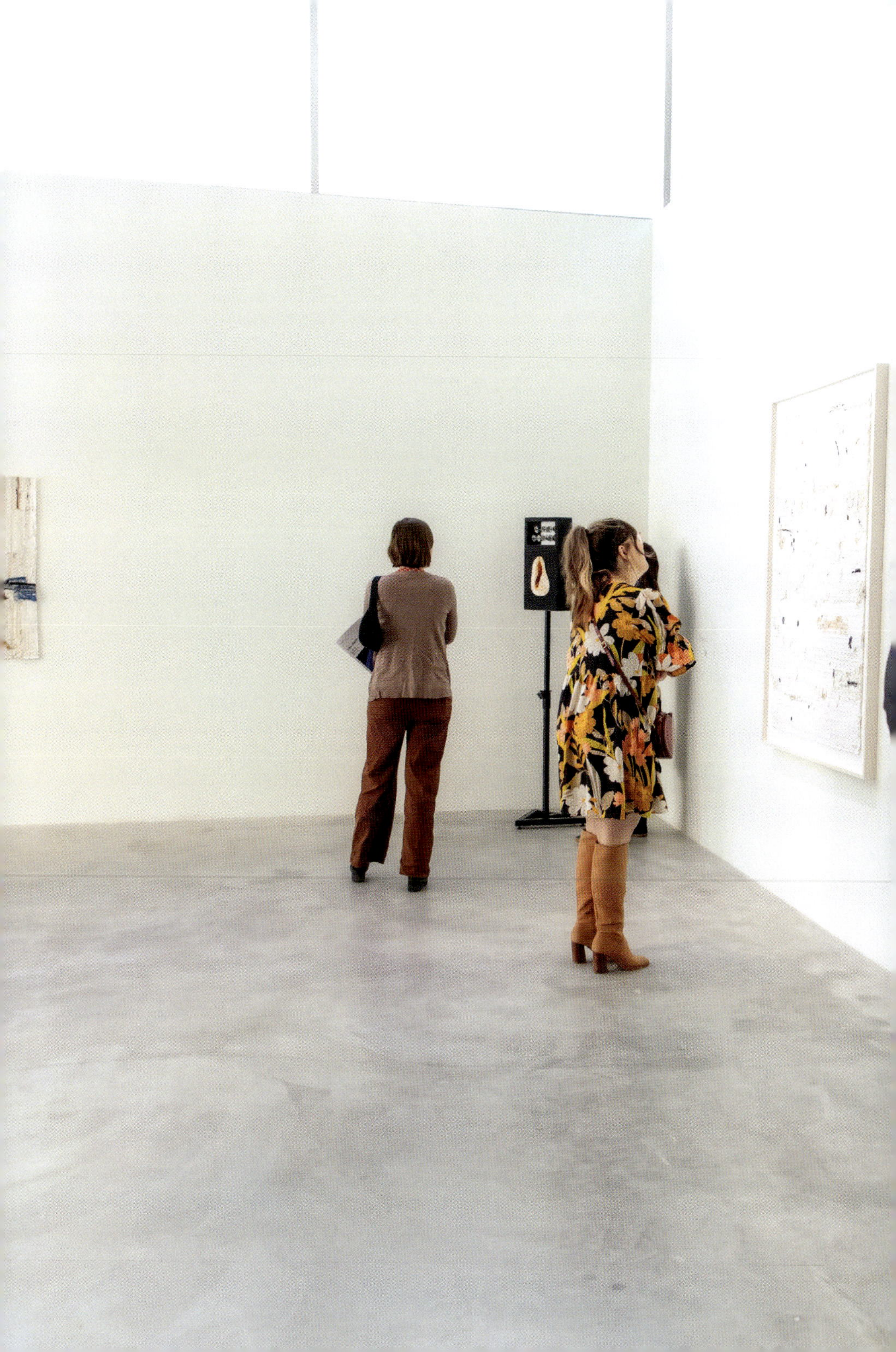

BIOGRAPHIES

JAMAL CYRUS (b. 1973, Houston, TX. Lives and works in Houston) is a multidisciplinary artist whose conceptual and research-driven practice scours American history to better understand the cultural and national heritage of Black political movements, social justice, and transhistorical influences of African diasporas. Cyrus actively engages with cultural cross-pollination and hybridity across and between historical eras.

DEAN DADERKO is the Ferring Foundation Chief Curator at the Contemporary Art Museum St. Louis, and has presented solo exhibitions with artists including Teresa Baker, LaToya Ruby Frazier, Joan Jonas, Ad Minoliti, Nicolas Moufarrege, Gina Pane, Paul Ramírez Jonas, and Haegue Yang, among many others. Daderko is a member of the Advisory Board of Denniston Hill, an artist residency in Glen Wild, New York.

SIMONE FATTAL (b. 1942, Damascus, Syria. Lives and works in Paris, France) studied philosophy at the École des Lettres in Beirut and the Sorbonne in Paris, and returned to Beirut, Lebanon in 1969. In 1980, fleeing the Lebanese Civil War, she settled in California and founded the Post-Apollo Press, a publishing house dedicated to innovative and experimental literary work. In 1988, she began making ceramic sculptures at the Art Institute of San Francisco, a practice she continues to the present.

DIONNE LEE (b. 1988, New York City, NY. Lives and works in Columbus, OH) uses photography, collage, and video to explore aspects of power, survival, and personal history relative to the American landscape. Lee received an MFA from California College of the Arts in 2017, was an Artist-in-Residence at The Chinati Foundation and Unseen California in 2022, and is the recipient of a 2025 Guggenheim Fellowship.

CANDICE LIN (b. 1979, Concord, MA. Lives and works in Los Angeles, CA) is an interdisciplinary artist who works with installation, drawing, video, and living materials and processes, such as mold, mushrooms, bacteria, fermentation, and stains. Her work deals with the politics of representation, as well as issues of race, gender, and sexuality by exploring varied histories of colonialism and diasporic life.

BEATRIZ SANTIAGO MUÑOZ's (b. 1972, San Juan, Puerto Rico. Lives and works in San Juan) approach to films and video making resembles the careful approach of an ethnographer. As she delves into cultural histories and local mythologies, she learns about and from the individuals who are both subjects and actors in her works. Across moving images, Santiago Muñoz traces the contours of cultural memory to reframe political and social issues.

VIVIAN SUTER (b. 1949, Buenos Aires, Argentina. Lives and works in Panajachel, Guatemala) was born in Buenos Aires in 1949 to exiled European parents. When she was twelve, during the Peròn regime, her family relocated to Basel, Switzerland, where she studied painting. In 1983, Suter settled in Panajachel, Guatemala, near Lake Atitlan. The local atmosphere, climate, vegetation, and animals became central concerns in her work, and she fosters a symbiotic relationship with her tropical environment.

EXHIBITION CHECKLIST

Jamal Cyrus

Untitled, 2021
Ink on board
6 × 14 inches
Collection of the artist

baía de todos os santos, 2022
Reclaimed wood, tambourine zills
Dimensions variable
Courtesy the artist and Inman Gallery, Houston, TX

Be as a stranger or traveler (Make Me a Pallet on the Floor), 2022
Denim, cotton thread, cotton batting, glue, earth, burlap
4 × 72 × 48 inches
Courtesy the artist and Inman Gallery, Houston, TX

Blue Alluvial Glue 1 (Shape), 2022
Denim, cotton thread, cotton batting
56 × 42 inches
Collection of the Modern Art Museum of Fort Worth, Gift of the Director's Council and Museum Purchase, 2022

Blue Alluvial Glue 2 (Line), 2022
Denim, cotton thread, cotton batting, metal
42 ½ × 55 inches
Collection of the Modern Art Museum of Fort Worth, Gift of the Director's Council and Museum Purchase, 2022

Blue Alluvial Glue 3 (Timbre), 2022
Denim, cotton thread, cotton batting, metal, fragments of vinyl records
55 × 42 ½ inches
Courtesy Katharine Barthelme Frank and Shane Frank

Sstrum, 2022
Helmet conch shell, wood, carpet, speaker stand, tambourine zills, corn grits, India ink
75 × 18 × 15 inches
Courtesy the artist and Inman Gallery, Houston, TX

Preparation for Extended Registers, 2024
Saxophone, cement, railway tie, wood
8 × 34 × 14 inches
Collection of Rona and Jeff Citrin

Horn Beam Sacrament, 2025
Sawhorses, custom-made steel and wood smoker, tenor saxophone, gauze, Mississippi River mud, sargassum, railroad spike, hardwood charcoal, cherry and hickory wood chips, and residues from Mississippi River Water, aloe, Twinkle silver polish, oud, frankincense, and myrrh
42 × 35 3/4 × 25 3/4 inches

Horn Beam Sacrament
Performance, 2025
Contributors: Jamal Cyrus, K. Curtis Lyle, Corey De'Juan Sherrard, Jr., and Damon Smith
Commissioned by the Contemporary Art Museum St. Louis

Watch a recording of Jamal Cyrus's *Horn Beam Sacrament*

Simone Fattal

Djet, 1988
Glazed stoneware
11 1/8 × 3 1/2 × 3 1/2 inches
Collection of Kathleen Frumkin and George Lakoff

Dueña, 1988
Glazed stoneware
10 3/4 × 3 3/16 × 3 3/16 inches
Collection of Kathleen Frumkin and George Lakoff

Goddess of the Springing Water, 1988
Glazed stoneware
13 1/2 × 3 1/2 × 3 1/2 inches
Collection of Kathleen Frumkin and George Lakoff

Good Tidings, 1988
Glazed stoneware
10 1/4 × 1 1/2 × 1 1/2 inches
Collection of Kathleen Frumkin and George Lakoff

Fix Your Gaze on Saturn's Rings, 2012–2022
Bronze
25 1/2 × 19 11/16 × 15 3/4 inches
Courtesy the artist and kaufmann repetto, Milan and New York

Le Grand Renversement 1948 [The Great Reversal 1948], 2012
Collage
45 × 38 inches
Courtesy the artist and Karma International, Zurich

Fish, 2015
Glazed stoneware
14 9/16 × 6 1/4 × 3/4 inches
Courtesy the artist and Karma International, Zurich

At the Pool, 2015
Collage on cardboard
23 × 29 inches
Courtesy the artist and kaufmann repetto, Milan and New York

Lucrecia, 2015
Collage on card
19 $\frac{3}{4}$ × 27 $\frac{1}{4}$ inches
Courtesy the artist and kaufmann repetto, Milan and New York

Untitled, 2017
Glazed stoneware
9 $\frac{1}{2}$ × 16 $\frac{1}{8}$ × 11 $\frac{3}{8}$ inches
Courtesy the artist and kaufmann repetto, Milan and New York

Ksar, 2018
Stoneware
9 $\frac{1}{10}$ × 13 $\frac{3}{4}$ × 12 $\frac{3}{16}$ inches
Courtesy the artist and kaufmann repetto, Milan and New York

Standing Figure IV, 2019
Stoneware
13 × 4 $\frac{1}{2}$ × 4 inches
Collection of Carol Greene, New York

Man and Wife (wife), 2021
Glazed stoneware
17 $\frac{3}{8}$ × 2 $\frac{3}{4}$ × 1 $\frac{11}{16}$ inches
Courtesy the artist and kaufmann repetto, Milan and New York

Initiation II, 2021
Glazed stoneware
26 × 10 $\frac{5}{8}$ × 9 $\frac{1}{16}$ inches
Courtesy the artist and kaufmann repetto, Milan and New York

Wave, 2023
Glazed stoneware
4 × 12 × 13 inches
Collection of Carol Greene, New York

Dionne Lee

Breaking Wave, 2018
Pigmented inkjet print
9 × 13 inches
Courtesy the artist and P.Bibeau, New York

Untitled, 2023
Gelatin silver print on handmade paper, divining rod
8 × 10 inches approximately
Courtesy the artist and P.Bibeau, New York

Currents, 2024
Single-channel video (black and white, silent)
18:51 minutes
Courtesy the artist and P.Bibeau, New York

Untitled, 2024
Single-channel video (black and white, silent)
2:03 minutes
Courtesy the artist and P.Bibeau, New York

Untitled Rock Drawing III (1), 2024
Gelatin silver print
10 × 8 inches
Courtesy the artist and P.Bibeau, New York

Untitled Rock Drawing III (2), 2024
Gelatin silver print
10 × 8 inches
Courtesy the artist and P.Bibeau, New York

Untitled Rock Drawing III (3), 2024
Gelatin silver print
10 × 8 inches
Courtesy the artist and P.Bibeau, New York

Untitled Rock Drawing V, 2024
Gelatin silver print
10 × 8 inches
Courtesy the artist and P.Bibeau, New York

Untitled Rock Drawing VI, 2024
Solarized gelatin silver print
10 × 8 inches
Courtesy the artist and P.Bibeau, New York

Walking Stick IV, 2024
Single-channel video (black and white, silent)
10:26 minutes
Courtesy the artist and P.Bibeau, New York

Candice Lin

La Charada China, 2018/2025
Earth, red clay, guano, cement, poppyseeds, sugarcane, seeds of various poisonous Caribbean plants, grow light, Mylar, wooden and metal armature, soaker hoses, irrigation system, tinctures in glass bottles, ceramics, toy boat, gourds, pencil on paper drawings, teapots, teacups, photographs, dried flora, chain, hardware, audio (11:47 minutes)
Courtesy the artist and François Ghebaly, Los Angeles and New York

Beatriz Santiago Muñoz

Otros usos [Other Uses], 2014
Single-channel video (color, sound)
6:52 minutes
Courtesy the artist and Sociedad del Tiempo Libre, San Juan, Puerto Rico

Pájaro, cómeme (Filoctetes) [Bird, Eat Me (Philoctetes)], 2023
Three-channel video (black and white and color, sound)
6:44 minutes
Courtesy the artist and Sociedad del Tiempo Libre, San Juan, Puerto Rico

Vivian Suter

No title, n.d.
85 acrylic on canvas paintings, hardware
Dimensions variable
Courtesy the artist and Gladstone Gallery, New York

Like Water is organized for the Contemporary Art Museum St. Louis by Dean Daderko, Ferring Foundation Chief Curator, with support from Grace Early, Exhibitions Assistant.

Like Water is the second in a series of four exhibitions collectively entitled *The Weather Inside*. The first exhibition in the series, entitled *Ecstatic Land*, was co-curated by Daderko with Daisy Nam for Ballroom Marfa in Marfa, Texas. It included artworks by Laura Aguilar, Genesis Báez, Teresa Baker, Dineo Seshee Bopape, Christie Blizard, Frank Duncan, Nancy Holt, Katherine Hubbard, Isuma, Benny Merris, Alan Michelson, Laura Ortman, Elle Pérez, Sondra Perry, and David Benjamin Sherry.

Major support for *Like Water* is provided by The Andy Warhol Foundation for the Visual Arts. This exhibition is generously supported in part by Étant donnés, a program of Villa Albertine; Independent Curators International; Alison Sieloff and Sam Foxman; Emily Rauh Pulitzer; Ann R. Ruwitch and John Fox Arnold; Mary Ann and Andy Srenco; Pat Whitaker and Dick Miles; and Whitaker Foundation.

ISBN: 978-0-9977364-8-9

Available through D.A.P./Distributed Art Publishers
75 Broad Street, Suite 630, New York, NY 10004
212.627.1999
artbook.com

Produced by Marquand Books, Seattle
marquandbooks.com

Edited by Dean Daderko and Grace Early
Designed by Ryan Polich
Proofread by Grace Early and Kathleen Garrett
Printed and bound in St. Louis by The Advertisers Printing Company

Front cover: *Blue Alluvial Glue 1 (Shape)*, 2022. Denim, cotton thread, cotton batting, 56 × 42 inches. Collection of the Modern Art Museum of Fort Worth, Gift of the Director's Council and Museum Purchase, 2022. Courtesy the Modern Art Museum of Fort Worth. Photo: Kevin Todora.

Back cover: *Like Water*, installation views, Contemporary Art Museum, St. Louis, March 7–August 10, 2025. Photo: Izaiah Johnson.

pp. 2–3, 4, 6, 10, 18, 28–29, 32–33, 37, 50–51, 54–57: *Like Water*, installation views, Contemporary Art Museum St. Louis, March 7–August 10, 2025. Photo: Izaiah Johnson.

pp. 38–39: Dionne Lee, *Untitled*, 2024. Installation view, *Like Water*, Contemporary Art Museum St. Louis, March 7–August 10, 2025. Photo: Izaiah Johnson.

p. 53: Vivian Suter, installation view, *Like Water*, Contemporary Art Museum St. Louis, March 7–August 10, 2025. Photo: Izaiah Johnson.